"WONDERFUL GOOD COOKING"

from
Amish Country Kitchens

G000039048

Photos and Amish Story
by Fred J. Wilson

Recipes Collected and Checked
by Larry Rogers

Johnny Schrock, Editor

HERALD PRESS
Scottdale, Pennsylvania
Kitchener, Ontario

ACKNOWLEDGMENTS

We thank those who helped provide information for this book and deeply appreciate the suggestions of persons who reviewed the manuscript.

Cover Photo — Young Amish boy does spring plowing with horse team.
Page 3 — Typical Amish children entertain themselves at a farm sale.

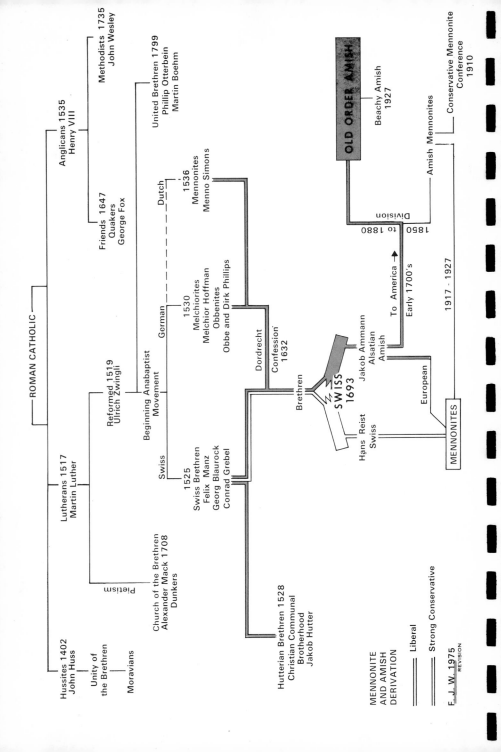

MENNONITE
AND AMISH
DERIVATION

E. J. W. 1975
REVISION

Liberal
Strong Conservative

ROMAN CATHOLIC

Hussites 1402
John Huss

Unity of
the Brethren

Moravians

Lutherans 1517
Martin Luther

Anglicans 1535
Henry VIII

Methodists 1735
John Wesley

Friends 1647
Quakers
George Fox

United Brethren 1799
Phillip Otterbein
Martin Boehm

Pietism

Church of the Brethren
Alexander Mack 1708
Dunkers

Reformed 1519
Ulrich Zwingli

Beginning Anabaptist
Movement

Swiss

German

Dutch

1525
Swiss Brethren
Felix Manz
Georg Blaurock
Conrad Grebel

1530
Melchiorites
Melchior Hoffman
Obbenites
Obbe and Dirk Phillips

1536
Mennonites
Menno Simons

Dordrecht
Confession
1632

Hutterian Brethren 1528
Christian Communal
Brotherhood
Jakob Hutter

Brethren

SWISS
1693

Jakob Ammann
Alsatian
Amish

Hans Reist
Swiss

To America

Early 1700's

European

1917 - 1927

MENNONITES

Amish Mennonites

OLD ORDER AMISH

Beachy Amish
1927

Conservative Mennonite
Conference
1910

1850 to 1880
Division

Introduction

The Amish, a rural people, are a part of the German-Swiss heritage called the "Pennsylvania Dutch." Amish women tend their kitchen gardens for their fresh vegetables. The fertile fields of the Amish farms raise the livestock for their meats, fresh country butter, milk, and eggs. Over wood-burning cast-iron stoves, the Amish cook prepares wholesome meals of real country cooking for her large family. It is not unusual for 15 to 18 to sit down around the big kitchen table for three meals a day.

Country cooking as found mostly in the Amish country is becoming a thing of the past. Many Amish cooks are sharing for your enjoyment their recipes, portioned for smaller families and modern stoves. It may surprise you to learn that some of your favorite dishes were Amish.

The Amish story and pictures are to enrich your appreciation of their cooking. Eating their style food and learning their way of life bring an appreciation for the Amish as a people. The Amish with their unusual dress and rejection of modern conveniences are looked upon by outsiders as a curiosity, instead of the stalwart, friendly people they really are. The Amish do not permit the taking of their pictures, according to the second commandment (Exodus 20:4). Our candid pictures are not meant to be personal photos of any one individual, but to help create a better understanding of these people. Also, the names used are common among the Amish and do not refer to any specific individual.

The Amish do not write about themselves, as they shun publicity. Those who have left the Amish sect can best verify the accuracy of the writings about them. One of these is Johnny Schrock, son of an Amish bishop, who suggested this book. "I was Amish for 24 years," he will tell you. Johnny has left the Amish but the Amish has never left him. "I am never ashamed to say I was born and raised Amish. They have put a lot of qualities in me that have stuck with me through the years and have helped me in life." In his respect and admiration for his heritage he has been most helpful in writing the story.

He still lives among the Amish in the largest settlement of them in the world, Holmes County, Ohio. Here live the most conservative Amish, the Old Order or "House Amish," so called because of their practice of holding church in members' homes or barns. There are several different sects among the Amish whose practices may vary from the Old Order group, and in other locations, local customs will vary.

Our Ohio Amish live in a community relatively unspoiled by the commercialization of the Amish sect. On many of the country roads, back off the main highways in the rolling green hills, the quiet is broken occasionally by the moo of a cow or horses' hooves on the gravel road as a buggy goes by. In the tranquil countryside the Amish live and enjoy the harvest of their labors and the peace and quiet of homes undisturbed by outside influences.

Relax and enjoy the Amish recipes from your kitchen. In the quiet of your home and the fellowship of your family you will say like the Amish, "Wonderful good food! Eat up."

Fred J. Wilson

Who Are the Amish?

In Millersburg, Ohio, in the heart of the Ohio Amish country, a horse and buggy pulls into a parking space. A man in a broad-brimmed hat steps out. He has no moustache with his untrimmed beard. He is dressed in a plain shirt — no pocket — and broadfall pants — barn-door style, similar to sailor pants. His suspenders are leather or cloth — no elastic. He hitches the horse to the meter pole and puts a coin in the meter. The woman then emerges, stepping down without his help. She wears her traditional black bonnet, a long plain dark blue dress with matching apron. With purse and shopping bag in hand she follows her husband as they walk to the store.

The Amish are easily recognized by their clothing style. A visitor asks, "Who are the Amish?" Their way of life is frequently misunderstood and many misconceptions about them are repeated so often that these are accepted as fact. We hope this book will give a better understanding and will encourage the reader to do further reading (some books for further reading are recommended on page 40).

The Amish, one of the "Plain People" and a sect of the Mennonites, are a rural people. Holmes and Wayne counties, with two thirds of the 133 church districts in Ohio, have the largest Amish population in the world. Nearby Tuscarawas, along with Stark, Geauga, Ashland, Defiance, Medina, Washington, Logan, Knox, Madison, and Hardin counties, all have one or more Amish settlements. The second largest Amish population is in Pennsylvania with 105 districts and the third is in Indiana with 88 districts. Smaller settlements are located in Illinois, Iowa, Tennessee, Wisconsin, Maryland, Delaware, Michigan, Oklahoma, Minnesota, Virginia, New York, Kansas, Missouri, and Kentucky. Outside the United States there are groups in Ontario and parts of South and Central America.

The Amish are direct descendants of the Anabaptists (rebaptizers) who appeared as a "Free Church" movement (1525-1536) during the Reformation. They were persecuted by both the major state churches, Roman Catholic and Protestant. Many of their leaders suffered martyrdom. Accounts of the torture and death of these devoted Christians are recorded in the *Martyrs Mirror*, written in 1659, and next to the Bible the book most read by the Amish.

The Swiss Brethren in Switzerland and Mennonites — named for a converted Roman Catholic priest, Menno Simons — emerged as the two principal Anabaptist groups. A third branch of the movement, the Hutterian Brethren, is the only Christian communal group to survive for

Page 6 — A beautiful flower garden is an Amish woman's joy. The small building is a "Daudy House."

400 years. Their colonies are located in Northwestern U.S. and Southwestern Canada.

Jakob Ammann, a conservative Swiss Anabaptist and church elder, from 1693 until his split with the church in 1697, insisted on very strict conformity to certain ritualistic and social practices. For unrepentant sinners Ammann demanded shunning by complete excommunication. This ban, as it was called, involved all social and business contacts, including those with his family. Even marital relations were to be suspended. The ban could be lifted upon public repentance and consent of the church body. Some Mennonite churches and the Amish still practice shunning.

The followers of Ammann became known as the Amish. He introduced foot washing into the communion service among the Swiss Brethren and changed its observance from once to twice yearly — spring and fall. He taught that trimming the beard was wrong and advocated uniformity in dress. All who disagreed with him, including Anabaptists who attended state churches, were to be excommunicated.

At the invitation of William Penn the Amish migrated to the United States in the early 1700s, along with the Mennonites and other religious groups escaping persecution in Europe. They first settled in Pennsylvania in what is now the Berks County area. The search for farmland took them westward to settlements in Ohio and Indiana.

In Europe the Amish have been assimilated into other groups, so today this unusual society exists only in America. The religious haven promised by Penn has not been perfect but has permitted the Amish to live according to their beliefs and to grow. The Amish are a distinctive minority in our America.

Nonconformity

"Be not conformed to this world: but be ye transformed by the renewing of your mind, that ye may prove what is that good, and acceptable and perfect, will of God."
Romans 12:2

Nonconformity for the Amish means a definite separation between the church and the world. Free association of the church members with a world of different value standards and beliefs will undermine the church. The uniformity of dress, horse-and-buggy transportation, marriage within the church fellowship, limited education in Amish schools — all these are a part of the separation doctrine. The Amish give daily expression to their piety in the world in observing these practices.

Nonresistance

"I say unto you, That ye resist not evil: but whosoever shall smite thee on thy right cheek, turn to him the other also." Matthew 5:39 (Read also Matthew 5:38-42; John 18:36; and Romans 12:19-21.)

The Amish believe a Christian does not use violence either in war or self-defense. They will suffer an injury rather than protect themselves by physical force. They will suffer loss rather than go to law. "Defenseless Christians" is a name given to all Anabaptist groups because of their refusal to fight back.

Brotherhood of Believers

"If any provide not for his own, and specially for those of his own house, he hath denied the faith, and is worse than an infidel." 1 Timothy 5:8

The only offering taken in church is at the end of the communion service. It is called "alms" and is used for the poor and church members suffering misfortune. The mutual aid fund for disaster help is raised through assessment based on the value of a member's real estate. The barn-raising is the most dramatic example of helping a brother recover from disaster. The Amish believe the Christian community is responsible for the care of the aged, poor, and sick. They have sought, with help from non-Amish friends, and have been granted exemption from compulsory insurance such as Social Security. The Amish never go on welfare.

Scriptural Authority

"All scripture is given by inspiration of God, and is profitable for doctrine, for reproof, for correction, for instruction in righteousness...." 2 Timothy 3:16

The Bible is the only scriptural authority and its teachings are accepted literally. The Bible is read in the home and in the school, but any interpretation of the Scriptures is left to the ministry of the church. Scriptural bases for many Amish practices are scattered through this book.

Ordnung

Each church has a number of unwritten rules called the *Ordnung*. The rules include many issues not covered in the Scriptures such as pleats in dresses, size and shape of men's hats, usage of new farm equipment, and electrical systems on buggies. The *Ordnung* is reviewed at a special service, sometimes called a council meeting, two weeks before Communion Sunday. After oral presentation of the rules by the ministers, they are discussed and voted on for approval. The vote must be almost unanimous. Approval means unity in the church and clears the way for the observance of communion. The Amish are bound together within their community in a relationship of goodwill toward all members cemented by the teaching of the Bible and the *Ordnung*.

Church

Andy Beachy finished sweeping the straw from the barn thrashing floor. Levi and John Beachy pull the bench wagon to the door. Each church district has its own specially built wagon to transport the church benches. The boys open the rear door of the wagon, unload the benches, and carry them inside. Here they line up the backless benches in rows on each side of the barn in preparation for tomorrow's church service. The men and women will sit on opposite sides and face each other. Between the two groups at one end, table and chairs are placed for the bishop, ministers, and deacon. Two boys are needed to carry in the wooden boxes of hymnals.

The last time the Beachys had church was in the winter and the service was held in the house. Furniture was moved to the porch to provide space for the benches. Many Amish homes are large and some have partitions or doors that can be moved to open the whole downstairs for the service.

The Beachys are members of Old Order or "House Amish." A church service is held every other week and each member of the district takes his turn in hosting the service. The church district is like a parish with about 20 to 30 families living in the same area. As a church grows to about 150 persons — usually too many for one home — a new district is started. The number of districts can be a guide to the population distribution of the Amish.

The district leader and administrator is the bishop. He may serve more than one district. The other ordained men are the two ministers or preachers and the deacon. All serve without pay for life. Their

Page 10 — In Amish country one sees many horse-drawn buggies.

Page 11 — The funeral service in the barn is over and the coffin is carried to the wagon for burial in a family plot.

12

calling requires no formal training. Each man agrees when he enters the church membership to accept if he is chosen to serve. Each woman agrees to serve as the wife of a minister if her husband is chosen.

As in the early church, the leaders are chosen by lot. "*And they prayed, and said, Thou, Lord, which knowest of all men, shew whether of these two thou has chosen. . . . And they gave forth their lots; and the lot fell upon Matthias; and he was numbered with the eleven apostles.*" Acts 1:24 and 26. At the Ordnungsgemee, or preparatory service, names for the lot are submitted by all members. Men receiving two or more votes are included in the lot. This may involve over a dozen men. Bibles or hymnals, all of similar appearance, one for each person in the lot, are placed on a table. Each passes by, picking up a book. One at a time the bishop opens the books until the one is found in which a slip of paper had been placed. The lot has fallen upon this man. An ordination service follows. Newly ordained persons are given a reasonable time to become familiar with their new responsibilities before assuming duties.

Lack of training is not a handicap. The Scripture says, "*And I will give you pastors according to mine heart, which shall feed you with knowledge and understanding.*" *Jeremiah 3:15 (cf. Jer. 26:2; 1 Pet. 4:11).* Each has faith that God will speak through him.

The minister's responsibilities are to preach and interpret the Bible to the congregation; to lead in prayer by reading from the prayer book; to serve the wine at communion; to visit the sick, widows, and orphans; and to assist in marriage and burial.

The deacon reads the Scripture; provides bread and wine for communion; brings in and pours the water into the cupped hands of the bishop at baptism; looks after temporal affairs of the members in hardship from illness, fire, and other mishaps; suggests to members who let their property deteriorate that this reflects on the Amish community; and assists young people in marriage arrangements.

The bishop, chosen by lot from among the ministers, is the only one who baptizes, marries, buries, and serves communion. He can expel sinners or receive back repentant members. He is recognized as the shepherd of the group. By congregational vote he controls clothing style, use of machinery, and other rules of the *Ordnung.*

The regular Sunday preaching service or *Gemee* is the basic service and is varied for special services such as communion, baptism, marriage, and funeral.

The Beachys will furnish and serve the meal to the members after the service. The menu is fixed by custom and will vary in some districts. For this Sunday there is bread, peanut butter, jelly, cheese,

Page 14 — Maple sap is gathered for the annual sugaring in the spring.

13

Trail Bologna, and coffee. The food is prepared the day before, except for the coffee.

The families arrive before the 9:00 a.m. service. Parking is no problem. The horses are unhitched and tethered together in a shady spot and the buggies are lined up in a field.

The men get together for small talk. Each wears his dark blue serge *Mutze* suit. The suit has no lapels and uses hooks and eyes for fastening instead of buttons. The *Mutze* has a split tail to signify that the wearer is a baptized member. The ladies wear black dresses with shoes and hose to match. On their heads are traditional black bonnets. A bow under each chin reveals that the white prayer cap is being worn under the bonnet. The children are miniatures of the adults.

As the time for the service draws near, the ordained men enter the barn first. The other men follow, the oldest first and the unmarried boys last. The women enter according to age, the young unmarrieds last. The sexes sit separately at opposite sides of the barn facing each other. The ordained men, seated at one end, face the congregation.

The *vorsinger*, or song leader, a male member, sounds the first few notes and then all join in in a slow chanting tune. As the singing begins the ordained men leave the service to meet in the house for *abrot*. Here the details of the morning service are discussed; the order for speaking arranged.

The singing continues. All hymns are from the *Ausbund*, a 400-year-old hymnal written in German. The thick book contains only the words of the hymns. There is no printed music; the hymns must be learned by ear. Musical instruments and singing in harmony are not permitted. The slow-moving tunes are dirgelike.

The second hymn in each Amish service is *Das Loblied No. 131* on page 770 in the *Ausbund*. This is known as the "Loob" or "Love" song. "*O Gott Vater, wir loben dich*" — "*O God, our Father, Thee we praise*," four stanzas of seven lines each. Eighteen to twenty minutes is required to sing the entire hymn through once. Fast tunes are worldly; the more conservative the church, the slower the singing.

The last hymn ends and the ordained men return. A 20-to-30-minute sermon opens the service. The group kneels and a silent prayer follows. All arise after prayer to hear the deacon read the Scripture. The congregation sits down for the main sermon, delivered by the bishop or one of the ministers. The sermon, lasing 45 minutes to an hour, is given in German without use of notes. During the sermon a chapter of the Bible is read.

Page 15 — The typical Amish farm with main house and a smaller "Daudy House" alongside. A big barn, many outbuildings, and a windmill are part of a good Amish farm.

The sermon over, the speaker asks for "*Zeugniss*" of the other ministers present or a layman. This is testimony that the Word of God has been presented faithfully in the sermon. This may take another twenty minutes. Prayer follows with the congregation kneeling. The prayer is read from the prayer book. The only time prayer is audible is when it is read. The congregation rises after prayer (one never sits down directly from a kneeling position), a closing hymn is sung, and the benediction given. The service has lasted about three hours.

There is time to stretch while the meal is readied. The older people are seated first, the men at one table and the women at another. Many stay after the meal to visit. Families leave as time for the evening chores nears. The young people stay for the evening singing.

Church benches are loaded back into the wagon for the next service in two weeks.

Baptism

Only the baptized enter the full fellowship of the church. Adult baptism is the major tenet of the Anabaptist churches. The Amish believe that only an adult can make the necessary commitment to follow the way of Jesus Christ, a step to be taken with full understanding of the consequences. Through special sermons and parents' help, young people are encouraged to join the church. Only members can be married in the church. Baptism is a commitment also to the Amish way of life.

Instruction is given to the young applicants. It is called "*dis Gemee Nooch geh*" or "to follow the church." Similar to catechism, the class meets for several weeks with the ministers during the *abrot*. The congregation must give approval for a new member to be accepted into the fellowship.

On baptism Sunday, the class is seated in a special group in front of the ordained in the center of the church. The applicants enter from the *abrot* before the ordained.

After the long sermon, the applicants kneel. The bishop asks each a few simple questions. A prayer is read from the book. The deacon's wife assists by removing the black caps of the kneeling girls. The bishop lays his hands on the applicant's head and cups them. The deacon dips a tin cup into a pail of water and pours the water into the bishop's hands. The water flows over the applicant's head as the bishop opens and closes his hands. The bishop baptizes, saying, "Upon your faith, you have confessed before God and these witnesses, you are baptized in the name of the Father, the Son and the Holy Spirit. Amen."

The bishop takes the right hand of each to welcome him into the church as he arises. A young man is given the holy kiss by the bishop.

17

A young woman's hand is placed in the hand of the minister's or deacon's wife, who gives her the holy kiss.

The bishop ends his sermon with remarks to the congregation about its responsibilities to the new members.

Ordnungsgemee

Closely following baptism Sunday is the *Ordnungsgemee*, the preparatory service for the communion service to follow.

The discussion and the acceptance of the *Ordnung* brings the membership into a unity of fellowship. Each member makes personal preparation to take communion, settling differences with other members and confessing his own faults. Communion is a cleansing time for the individual and the whole fellowship. *"But let a man examine himself, and so let him eat of that bread, and drink of that cup. For he that eateth and drinketh unworthily, eateth and drinketh damnation to himself. 1 Corinthians 11:28, 29.*

The need for an ordination is decided by a vote of the congregation at this service. Nominations for the lot are made at the communion service two weeks later.

Communion

Gross Gma, the communion service, is observed twice yearly. Differences have been settled. With the membership in accord, the most solemn and unifying experience of the church district takes place on this day.

Children do not attend this service or the preceding preparatory service. The Amish church is an adult fellowship. Only church members attend the all-day service.

Sermons are long, the main service lasting 1 1/2 to 2 hours. Members leave the service to eat and return. Near the end, the ministers bring in the wine and bread. The bread has been home-baked by the family hosting the service. The wine is also homemade either by the bishop's wife or another member. As the bishop explains the symbolism of the bread and wine, the bread is sliced on a table by his side. The deacon hands the bishop a slice of bread. With the membership standing, the bishop and one minister break off pieces of bread and give one to each member. As the bread is put into the mouth, each member bows at the knees and sits down. A cup from the kitchen cupboard is filled with wine. The members rise and the cup is passed. Each drinks from the common cup, again bows at the knees, and sits down.

Page 18 — A two-ton, 80-foot section of barn frame is in one piece, raised. Work started at 7:30 a.m. Over 600 men participated in the barn-raising during the day, finishing the job about 3:30 p.m.

Page 19 — Women watch from lawn of the house while waiting to serve a sumptuous noon meal. Note the straw shed to the right of the barn.

The *Zeugniss* (testimony) follows. Then the account of Christ washing the disciples' feet is read from John 13. Pails of water and towels are brought in by the deacon and laymen. Men and women go into separate rooms, where they remove their shoes and stockings. Pairing up with the next person, they stoop or kneel to wash each other's feet and dry them with a towel. After each pair have finished, they rise and give the holy kiss, a symbol of love and fellowship.

Schooling

Ever since opening their first school in 1925, the Amish have been at odds, at one time or another, with public school systems in the states where they live. They have had differences on standards of education, but are agreed on the need for schooling at the elementary level.

The U.S. Supreme Court handed down one of its far-reaching and historic rulings on May 15, 1972, when it declared in favor of the Amish in the case of the State of Wisconsin vs. Jonas Yoder, et al. Compulsory school attendance was the issue. The right of the Amish to maintain and operate their own schools according to their educational needs was established.

Chief Justice Burger, in delivering the opinion of the court, defined clearly the Amish values regarding the educational process as a part of the whole living experience. "We see that the record in this case abundantly supports the claim that the traditional way of life of the Amish is not merely a matter of personal preference, but one of deep religious conviction, shared by an organized group, and intimately related to daily living." He emphasized the constancy of the Amish to their convictions. "Aided by a history of three centuries as an identifiable religious sect and a long history as a successful and self-sufficient segment of the American society, the Amish in this case have convincingly demonstrated the sincerity of their religious beliefs, the interrelationship of belief with their mode of life."

The Amish have a definite educational goal: that is, to impart to their children the knowledge and abilities to be good productive Amish adults. The rewards of the Amish life are not here in this world but in God's eternity. The children's education must meet the demands of the Amish lifestyle. A separated society's needs are different from those of the world about them. They believe that many public school standards and subjects taught are not beneficial for the Amish, and at the high school level these are a threat to the Amish value standards.

In the United States 11,000 pupils are enrolled in 330 Amish schools that range in size from eight pupils to one with eighty-one

students taught by two teachers. Most are one-teacher schools with an average of thirty-three pupils. In some schools all the pupils may come from two or three families. Amish frequently attend rural public schools on the elementary level.

An Amish school serves a neighborhood or one or more church districts. The pupils walk to school. They carry lunch boxes, since there is no school lunch program. The building is designed and oriented to utilize the natural light, as there is no electricity. Schools are heated with an old-fashioned coal furnace or heater. A few have indoor lavatories; the majority still depend on an "outhouse." The drinking fountain is the yard pump. A school building valued at $20,000 is constructed by the men of the district at a cost for materials of perhaps $8,000 to $9,000. The same blueprints may be used for several schools. Classrooms are usually equipped with discarded public school desks. There is some nostalgia about the schools among older Americans who are reminded of the country schools they attended many decades ago.

The Amish school child spends five or six hours a day in school. Class may start at 9:00 a.m. and last until 4:00 p.m. with an hour off for lunch. The children play outside during the lunch hour and also during morning and afternoon recess periods. Those who remember the one-room school recall studying while another class recited. This time is also used to do the artwork or special papers that adorn the walls and windows of the schoolroom, giving it a cheerful air.

Attendance is at a high level — 90 percent or over. School may be closed for events in the community such as a corn husking, a wedding or a funeral. The lost time is made up, sometimes on Saturday, to meet the required number of school days per year. Amish schools are seldom closed because of snow in the winter, a reminder that walking and the horse and buggy have some advantages over buses.

In spite of the teachers' limited schooling, limited libraries and equipment, Amish pupils have good achievement records. In tests, compared with non-Amish in subjects stressed in the Amish school, their scores are on par or may excel. Considerable emphasis is given to memorization and factual material. Science and other subjects which encourage independent thinking are avoided. Right-and-wrong decisions are easier to make if based on memorized material. This is reflected in the Amish approach to biblical teachings.

Page 22 — An Amish boy takes over the reins of the team while his father loads hay. An Amish school is in background.

Page 23 — Grain is cut with an old horse-drawn reaper. Women and children will follow to stack it in the familiar field shocks of another generation.

Discipline is not a problem in the Amish school. The teacher is respected as an adult and is in control of the classroom. The Amish believe that only a few rules are needed for school but they should be rigidly enforced. Parental approval of the school discipline reinforces respect for the teacher.

One argument against the Amish school is lack of certified teachers. The teachers are a product of the Amish educational system with no more than eight years of schooling and no formal teacher training. They do not qualify for certification. Many come to the classroom equipped only with an invitation to teach from the school board. They are selected because the board believes they have the character and qualities wanted in a teacher. Teaching becomes a calling, not just a job. The Amish teacher is an adult exemplifying the faith, an example for children to admire and respect. The teacher is a part of the community and his life as a person is on view daily away from the school. What he does is more important than what he says.

Wages are low, ranging from $6 to $20 a day. Other jobs for the Amish in the area may pay two to three times as much. Teachers make sacrifices because they like to teach. They believe God has called them to teaching. Many say they find it rewarding to watch the growth of the children, and to prove themselves worthy of their responsibility.

Financial support comes from the church district or parents or both. School support plans vary from freewill giving, to assessment, to tuition. The cost to educate an Amish child may be one tenth that of the public school child. A local school board representing the church district administers the school. To coordinate and speak for Amish on matters of education with the state, organizations have been set up. In Ohio a 65-member Amish Committee oversees the schools. Pennsylvania has an Amish Church School Committee and Indiana, a State Board.

In addition to the three R's — readin', 'ritin', and 'rithmetic — spelling, English, and phonics are taught. Most schools teach German for Bible reading, since the spoken German or "Dutch" is not the written German. Some history and geography (using maps) is taught. Singing is a favorite activity, mostly German hymns. The use of German in speaking is limited. Skill in English usage is needed because homes use the "Dutch."

Bible reading is done in school to teach morality. Theology is left to the church. The Amish believe education should teach moral values and school textbooks are selected on this basis.

Formal education ends for the Amish at the eighth grade but the law requires attendance to age 16. To comply, various plans for vocational training have been worked out with local school authorities.

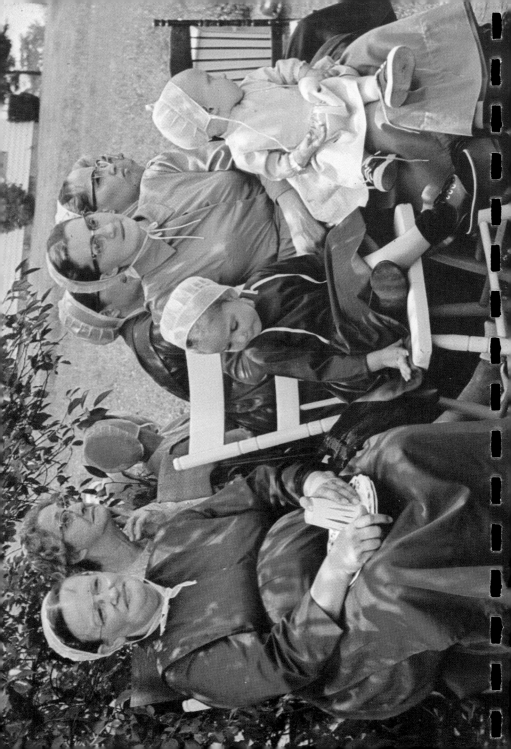

One is to hold class once a week for reporting and discussing assigned work projects. An Amish boy works on the farm under his father's supervision. He has special assignments, keeps notes, and makes a report to the school. A girl learns homemaking with her mother's teaching. These must not be home or farm chores but real learning experiences. Only the Amish can teach how to live the Amish life.

By today's standards the Amish may be considered backward in education. Their philosophy is consistent in developing a child to take his place in the Amish society and lifestyle.

Love and Marriage

Marriage, a sacred life relationship, is expected of young Amish people, with mates chosen within the Amish faith. The choice of a mate is a "love match"; parents do not arrange the marriage as it is sometimes thought. For a couple living together in an Amish home, raising a big family and working a large farm requires more than arrangement in marriage. Love does exist in the home, but it is not expressed publicly, not even a kiss or embrace in front of the children.

Sunday night after church the "singing" is held in the barn or house of the host family. Here the young can get together for singing the "fast tunes," playing mixer games, and some barn dancing. These socials keep the young people together to meet partners within the Amish sect. The natural teenage boy-girl relationships are directed inwardly.

Eli Miller has known Katie Yoder for as long as he can remember. Amish families with their close social and church ties are well acquainted and the children know each other from childhood. Eli remembers Katie as the girl he used to tease and later as the second baseman in the ball games at school.

But Katie looks different at this Sunday night "singing." She is dressed traditionally Amish like all the other girls. Her black prayer cap is set a little different over her strawberry blond hair and her plain yellow dress gives her a glow. Eli notices she is coming into womanhood.

Through custom and the natural shyness young Amish boys do not ask a girl directly for a date. A friend acts as the go-between and if the invitation is declined there is less embarrassment for each party. "Dan, ask Katie Yoder if I can drive her home tonight." Dan Erb, Eli's

Page 26 — Typical Amish women, young girls, and children resting and watching at a farm sale.

Page 27 — Farm talk by Amishmen at a machinery sale.

28

friend, has been eyeing Lizzie Mast, so the boys help each other. Both invitations are accepted.

Eli manages to drive Katie home for several Sunday evenings. After a few dates, they feel more comfortable with one another and meetings are arranged directly. Now their relationship is kept more secretive. Eli dresses up on Saturday evenings as if to go to town and spends the evening with her. They are seen together at work parties called "frolics," such as a corn husking, and socials, such as a barn dance or taffy pull.

The buggy rides home can be slow and meandering, leading to a quiet spot off a lane. The silence is broken only by the whinny of the horse answering the croak of a frog or the hoot of an owl. With moon and stars overhead, a boy and a girl can dream of their future together. With a battery radio, they may enjoy a little country-and-western music.

The horse needs little attention to finish the drive to Katie's home. The family are all in bed and Eli comes in to "stay awhile." Like all Amish homes the door is never locked and the family does not awaken. Katie and Eli have privacy to continue their courting.

"Bundling," the custom of courtship by lying in bed together fully clothed, is frequently associated by "outsiders" with the Amish. This practice predates the Amish by several centuries and was started in the British Isles and came to America with the early settlers. Supposedly, the lack of adequate heating made this way of courtship necessary. The practice is on the decline; Amish leaders frown on it and are ashamed to discuss it. Whether young Amish couples like Katie and Eli practice "bed courtship" depends on the couple.

After being steadies for some time, Katie and Eli become "promised" to each other. There is no ring for their engagement or public announcement. Couples always hedge on marriage plans until the banns are published in church, and their families are told only a few days before. For Eli and Katie it is about time for them to settle down. He is twenty-two and she, twenty, about average ages for an Amish marriage.

One evening Eli and Katie drive to Bishop Andy Raber's. He is pleased with the wedding plans and says, "You will be published next Sunday." The second Thursday following is chosen for the wedding day. Tuesdays and Thursdays are traditional wedding days and the popular season is fall or winter.

Katie makes her dress from the plain light blue cotton material she bought for her own and her attendants' dresses, along with white organdy for the aprons. Eli's mother recently made him a new *mutze* suit and collarless white shirt. The Amish bride and groom and their attendants all wear regular churchgoing clothes. The bride and groom each have two attendants called "nava huckers," a corruption of "nevvehocker."

Katie has a hope chest of linens and dishes. Her parents will give some things from the family larder. Eli's father will present him with a horse and some farm tools. With the money Eli has saved from his job, he and Katie can buy a bed, kitchen table, a few chairs, a stove, and a dish cupboard at a farm sale.

Invitations are sent out after the public announcement. Many of the guests will come from other Amish communities. Amish weddings may have two to three hundred guests.

Katie's family furnishes all the food, and uncles, aunts, and neighbors start the preparation several days in advance. The bride's home, where the meal is served, is filled with food, tables, and chairs on the wedding day.

The marriage service is at a neighbor's house. Arrangements are the same as for Sunday church with the furniture moved out of the way for the church benches. Two sets of three chairs facing each other are reserved for the wedding party in front of the ordained men.

On the wedding day everyone is up early, including Katie, to do the farm chores. Breakfast finished, she dresses for the wedding, slips into her new dress, puts on her new organdy prayer cap and apron. Katie has no special veil or bridal bouquet. Wedding rings are not given in the ceremony.

At the neighbor's house guests begin arriving for the 9:00 a.m. service. Horses are unhitched and put in the barn, and buggies are parked in the field. The men and women congregate in two separate groups. At nine o'clock all enter the service, the ordained men first, then the men, and the women last. Singing of the hymns begins and the ordained men leave. In an upstairs room, they meet with the bride and groom for Vermahuung or "exhortation." Final instructions are given on the duties of the husband and wife to each other in an Amish marriage.

As the last hymn finishes, the wedding party enters the room. The bride and her two attendants are seated on chairs in front and the groom's party faces them. The ordained men soon return and the service begins with Bishop Raber announcing, "Eli Miller and Katie Yoder were published to be married. If anyone has scriptural grounds why they should not be married, let him speak up now. If not, the service will proceed." The sermons start with the story of the creation, of the first man and wife, Adam and Eve, and the story of Ruth. The sermon emphasizes the responsibilities of married life. The love story of Tobias and Sarah in the apocryphal book of Tobit is told.

During the service, cooks at the Yoder home are busy getting ready for the wedding feast. Near the end of the morning's preaching, the cooks slip over to see the couple take their vows.

It is almost noon as the last sermon ends. Katie and Eli rise and stand before Bishop Raber. He asks them several questions: Do you agree on the Christian basis of marriage with one man and one woman? Do you accept each other for husband and wife? Will you care for each other in sickness? Do you agree that marriage can be dissolved only by death? Katie and Eli quietly answer "Yes" to each. Bishop Raber takes Katie's right hand and places it in Eli's hand praying: "Raquel took the hand of the daughter Sarah and put it into the hand of Tobias and said: 'The God of Abraham, Jacob, and Isaac be with you and help you together and give you His blessing richly over you,' . . . and all through Jesus Christ, our Lord and Savior. Amen." Looking at them he adds, "You are now man and wife and cannot be separated until death."

There is no kiss or embrace. The couple returns to their chairs by their attendants. The *Zeugniss* or testimony starts. A visiting bishop speaks and is followed by several others giving witness to a good Christian marriage. The service ends in a little over three hours with prayer and a hymn.

All move over to the Yoder home for the wedding dinner and festivities. The wedding party is driven in newly painted buggies the quarter mile to Katie's house by "hostlers," boys appointed to look after the wedding party for the day.

For the wedding dinner the wedding party is seated at a specially decorated corner or "eck." Katie's father shows the guests to their places. The marrieds are served first; the men in one room, the women in another or in the kitchen. The unmarrieds wait their turn and the children get their food and eat outside.

The wedding dinner is the most lavish meal of the Amish. There is an endless supply of golden-brown baked chicken, mashed potatoes, gravy, dressing, meat loaf, salads, cheese, fresh vegetables and fruits, jams, candies, decorated cakes and cookies, coffee, milk, iced tea, homemade schnitz, cherry, raisin, and pecan pies, and rich, creamy vanilla ice cream.

Katie and Eli open gifts while the tables are being prepared for the next group of diners. The gifts that are wrapped are in store paper. Gifts are practical such as kitchenware for the bride and tools or a milk pail for the groom. Each giver is thanked.

31

Hymns of a lighter variety are sung during the day. Guests have their small hymnals along and pick their favorites.

At the evening meal the "hostlers" mingle among the diners rattling a pot of coins at each man until he gives something. The repartee from reluctant givers adds to the frivolity. The "hostlers" are busy during the day arranging dates to pair up the unmarrieds at the late evening meal or "midnight table."

The day's activities wind down as the last guests leave. The bridal couple retires to the privacy of a room in the house. For the Amish there is no honeymoon, American-style. The new couple takes its place in the Amish community as married persons. Visitations will be made to relatives, spending a day or two at each home. Katie and Eli have started a new life together and they look forward to the blessing of a family "as the Lord will provide."

Death

"Not my will, but thine, be done." Luke 22:42

When death comes, the faith of the family carries the Amish through their suffering. The community relieves the family of details and makes all the funeral arrangements. The state requires embalming of the body, the one service a local funeral director performs. An Amish cabinet maker builds a six-sided coffin of plain varnished wood. The only hardware are the hinges at the center for the cover. Only the upper part of the deceased is shown. The body is dressed in regular church clothing. The coffin may be unlined or a plain white cloth may cover the plain wood interior.

Family friends dig the grave by hand. There are no flowers. Close friends and relatives hold a night-long wake. Before the 9:00 a.m. funeral, mourners gather at the house or barn of the deceased, maybe both. Over 1,000 mourners may come, and several services may be held at adjacent farms. The funeral service is shorter but similar to the regular Sunday service. One or more preachers officiate.

As each service finishes the mourners walk to the deceased's home, where the coffin is set on two sawhorses and each mourner takes a last look, women filing by one side and men the other. After the last mourner has passed, the coffin cover is closed and fastened with screws. It is covered with a tarpaulin and loaded on a horse-drawn spring wagon.

Horses and buggies are hitched up. The procession moves somberly to a small fenced family cemetery at a nearby farm.

Four men carry the coffin on two poles and place them over the grave. After the Scripture, a short prayer, and a hymn, the poles are removed and the coffin is gently lowered with webbing strips. Family friends shovel earth into the grave — earth to earth — completing the service. A mound of fresh earth, with a wooden marker at each end, identifies the plain grave. Later a small stone with name and birth and death dates may mark the grave.

The funeral meal is served at the home. Here visitors, some of whom have come long distances, socialize. Amish settlements depend for their news on a neighbor who will take "death messages" by phone. On receiving the news, a car or van and driver is hired or a bus chartered. Families are large and funerals are well attended. An obituary in the *Sugarcreek Budget* may read: "Dan Yoder 93, died. Surviving are 7 sons, 6 daughters. 90 grandchildren, 179 great-grandchildren," 282 in all. "Fannie Beachy 90, died. Surviving are 8 sons, 7 daughters, 94 grandchildren, 156 great-grandchildren and a number of great-great grandchildren, over 300 survivors."

Farm Sale

"Folks, here is a gasoline iron that works. Let's start it at five dollars. Five, do I hear five dollars? . . . One dollar, over here . . . one and a half . . . now two . . . two-fifty to you." The auctioneer points . . . a head nods. . . . From the rear of the crowd, "Two seventy-five" and the bidding settles down between two bidders.

"Four . . . four-fifty. . . . " Quickly, the auctioneer moves his head from bidder to bidder and the bid rises to nine dollars.

"Nine-fifty to you?" A moment's hesitation . . . a negative shake of the head. "Sold to Levi Hershberger."

The auctioneer's Amish clerk clarifies the name, "It is Levi B. Hershberger." There are nine other Levi Hershbergers; the middle initial is important. Levi's father's name was Ben and each of his children's middle initial is "B." Another Amish clerk in the house collects money for the purchases.

The Amish buy much of their household and farm equipment at these sales. Home articles are bought for utility, not style. Farm sales are fun. It's hard to resist trying for a bargain, rooting through goods spread out everywhere. There are tables of dishes to go over and "lots" of small articles in cartons such as kitchenware, clothing, dressmaking remnants, linens, books, hardware, tools, workshop cast-offs, and junk. I once saw a wastebasket sold complete with wastepaper!

The Amish like dishes, and young girls collect them for their "hope chests." Dishes and other household articles can be both useful and fancy such as homemade quilts, doilies, and table scarfs.

A rocking chair, a spacious painted cupboard, a sturdy worktable, and small articles such as an old-fashioned clock, an oil lamp, or a plant stand end up in Amish homes. At non-Amish farm sales electrical appliances go begging and outsiders may find a bargain. Picture frames are not popular because the Amish do not have wall pictures except on calendars. Amish rooms may have several calendars.

Eli Yoder is retiring from farming and his son John will take over the family farm. The older Yoders are moving into the *Grossdaadi Haus* or "daudy house," the home for the grandparents. This is a smaller house, either attached or a few feet from the big house. The son and his family will occupy the big house where he has room to raise his family. The moving is usually done in the winter or early spring before the fields are planted. During this season several Amish sales are held each week. Relatives often come for the sale from long distances and visit in the area.

The sale at Yoders is to sell excess farm stock, machinery, and household goods and to set a market value on the things son John buys from the family farm. Neighbors bring in consignment pieces to sell.

Sales may start at 9:00 or 10:00 a.m. and last till 4:00 or 5:00 p.m. In a vacant shed or in the basement of the house a lunch stand serves coffee, soft drinks, hotdogs, sloppy joes, milk, homemade pie, and candy bars. Sale furniture set out on the lawn is filled with chatting Amish onlookers. Buyers and spectators enjoy the festive occasion.

Weekly Sales

Amish farm products are sold in national markets. Merchants advertise "Amish Swiss Cheese from Holmes County, Ohio," or "Genuine Trail Bologna." Not so well known but more important to the Amish farmer is the weekly livestock and produce auction sale. Here the products of his farm reach the outside markets. In some settlements several sales on different days and locations bring the markets close to all the farmers.

The Amish farmer attends sales regularly and carefully notes the prices, the same as any good businessman. He may sell off some of his dairy herd or buy feeder stock to raise.

Sons are frequently seen with their fathers. Small fry enjoy a day "in town" and an ice-cream treat. The older boys learn the practical economics of marketing, a part of their ongoing education as a future Amish farmer.

The Amish woman and her daughters may take advantage of the trip to town to shop for staples, cloth, sewing supplies, shoes for the children, and other household articles.

Horse Sale

Amishmen and their sons crowd the sales arena for a horse sale. The horse is a symbol of the Amish way of life, a necessity for transportation and work. The first love of an Amishman is his family; his second love, his horse. A good horse is a luxury and a prestige symbol that is justified as useful. A trim buggy horse or a husky strong draft horse are bid up at sales and are prized possessions.

At a horse sale only horses and a few mules or ponies are sold. Animals are described according to the consignor's recommendations. Deliberate misrepresentation is not tolerated by buyers; his stock will not sell at future sales. Horses from recognized stock farms attract buyers and bring top prices.

A horse may be introduced as having "a ticklish behind, if given a loose tug" . . . or "a watery eye — he doesn't know it, so it doesn't bother him" . . . or "a family horse . . . traffic-safe . . . your wife can drive it." Buyers of a draft horse are told, "It will work either side and with a jockey stick."

To buyers of teams of horses, the auctioneer announces: "For you buyers a hitch wagon is in the back of the sale barn. Make your hitches early. No team can be returned after today." The privilege of trying out the team is part of the sale conditions. A work team is a big investment — like a new tractor to another farmer — except as one Amishman said, "The tractor don't give manure." A team that does not work together can be returned to the consignor.

Horse equipment, called tack, is sold before the horses. Tack may include harness, collars, work harness, and parts for harness and hitches. Saddles are not offered; the Amish do not have riding horses, except the young boys may occasionally ride bareback. An Amishman will say, "Horses are for work."

Barn-Raising

"Bear ye one another's burdens, and so fulfil the law of Christ." Galatians 6:2

Noah Troyer sits down in his spacious farm kitchen. His wife, Deana, is helping the ladies get the evening meal for the remaining workers. It has been a long and exciting day. Thankfully, Noah looks at the new barn. The new, raw wood siding glows a golden yellow in the late afternoon sun. A barn that was not there this morning! Waking in the night almost a month ago to the day, seeing the bright orange glow of the fire, hearing the frightened noises of the livestock is still a vivid memory. Today he might say, "It pleases me to be Amish."

His Amish brothers came to the smoldering mess the morning after the fire to help clean up.

Plans to rebuild were made. Jonas Miller's carpenter crew was hired to lay out and engineer the building of the new barn. Church appraisers examined the loss. The value was set and the church mutual assistance fund paid Noah three fourths of the appraisal. The church fund is collected from each family by the deacons, based on the value of their real-estate tax. The fund is for help in disasters, and assessments are made as often as needed.

The Amish barn is patterned after the Swiss bank barn. Building on a slope allows ground-level access to both floors, the thrashing floor above and animal stalls below. The typical barn is 40 feet wide and 60 to 80 feet long. Unique to the Amish is the straw shed. This is about as wide as the barn but shorter and is attached at the center of one side like the stem of a T. Thrashing is done on the upper floor and the straw blown into a straw pile in the shed. Trapdoors in the floor make dropping straw to the animal area easier. The bedding straw mixed with animal waste makes the fertilizer prized by the Amish farmer.

Logs for the heavy barn framing are cut from timber on the farm. Additional logs come from a friend's farm down the road. A portable, tractor-powered sawmill is set up in a field near the barn site. A tractor is not permitted for farming but can be used for belt power. The beams, posts, and rafters are sawed according to carpenter Miller's bill of materials. The frame takes about 50,000 feet of timber. Oak is best but other hardwoods are used. Green lumber is used because it is easier to cut. When the wood dries it will make the joints tight.

The wall of the lower level is concrete block. Each day Amish volunteers work to lay up the walls. The wall ends at the thrashing-floor level. Newly sawed floor beams, set on 10-inch square posts, are laid across the foundation wall. Floor joists cross the beams and rest on the wall.

The Miller crew is busy prefabricating the upper structure. Eight-inch-square posts and sills are mortised. The ends of beams are cut to tenons. Holes are precisely drilled in both for the wooden pins. When the joints are assembled, the tenons are inserted in the mortise sockets. The pins are driven into the holes, drawing the pieces together. Purlin beams are notched for the rafters. Braces are cut and fitted. After all the pieces are prepared, a horse and wagon haul them to the thrashing floor for assembly. A work platform is made of temporary planks laid over the joists. The frame parts are fitted together, using a sledge for stubborn pieces.

The raising sequence is planned, with the last piece of framework placed on the bottom. Connecting joints of completed frames are checked for fit. Wood siding is placed along the foundation, metal roofing is piled nearby, cartons of nails and baskets of homemade wooden pins are handy. All is ready for the raising.

The Amish community has been watching the construction progress. Word is passed. "The Troyer barn-raising is Saturday a week." Chores are done quickly that morning. Soon after daylight men begin to arrive with hammers and nail aprons. By 7:30 there are enough men to raise the first section. Before the day's work starts, carpenter foreman Miller talks to the workers in "Dutch," giving instructions for the day. He mixes in English, saying, "Be sure that you are not the one to cause an accident that will hurt someone else."

Each man is tensed, ready for the foreman's signal. It comes, "Hep-Hep," the rhythm of the motion starts. The frame is lifted by hand. As it is raised men move forward, jab a spike pole (a sapling with a spike in one end) into the frame and move it up to a vertical position. The post tenons drop into the sill mortises. The frame is kept in position with ropes tied to the top while temporary braces are nailed to the floor. Come early if you are invited to a barn-raising. The most interesting part is in the first hour as the frames go up into place.

Young Amishmen quickly climb the posts and rails. Using a sledge they drive the wood pins into the joints. By 8:30 a.m. all the heavy framing is in place. Purlins and rafters are about completed by 10:00 a.m. As each section of frame is placed, siding boards are nailed on. Other crews are working, one building doors, others below building animal stalls. On the roof, cross strips are nailed to the rafters for the metal roofing. The strips form a convenient ladder over the roof. By noon the frame is about finished and the siding on.

Noah's wife, Deana, and the women prepare the meal. All morning dishes of food arrive at the house. The serving table is set up under a tent on the lawn. Workers lay their hats in piles and wash in large basins and tubs. Each picks up a tray and files past long tables of chicken, dressing, homemade gravy, potatoes, salads, cooked and fresh vegetables, relishes, pie, coffee, and fruit drink. Church benches in the shade on the lawn serve as seats and tables. Men relax, talk, and enjoy the fellowship. The trays are returned clean with no food left on them. A clean plate is an example of Amish thrift. After the meal some workers leave. Soon it's back to work for others.

Metal roofing sheets are fastened down, a dozen men hammering in unison. The large barn doors are hung, the siding finished, the flooring laid, the granaries built, and the guttering hung. By 4:30 that same day hay is loaded on the upper floor and stock is bedded down below.

While Noah rests for a minute in his kitchen reflecting on the day, he thanks God for the blessing of the church fellowship. Over 400 men worked and over 100 women prepared the meal and served it. The children thought it was a big day with lots of excitement. A neighbor of Noah's, Al Weaver, summed it up, "It is wonderful that people can stick together and help each other. I hope they can always do this."

The Budget

No account of the Amish is complete without mentioning the *Budget*. The *Sugarcreek Budget*, as it is sometimes called, is a weekly newspaper printed in Sugarcreek, Ohio, in the Amish country and is the communication network for the "Amish-Mennonite Communities Throughout the Americas." The paper's publishers and Editor Sylvester Miller are non-Amish.

Budget seems an unlikely name for a newspaper until one consults the dictionary: "A budget — a bag or sack — a store or journal such as a budget of news." Truly the weekly *Budget* is a great mailbag in print. Reporters, or "scribes" as they are called, send in about 250 letters weekly with folksy news of their communities.

Their pay is a subscription to the paper. News reporting is faithful and regular.

"Troyer district church met at Andy Weavers with Fannie and Levi Zook visiting" . . . "Katie Yoder isn't well yet from her gallstone operation. She had four large stones" . . . "John Miller's had Sunday supper at Eli Hershberger's" . . . "A little 6 1/2 pound dishwasher came to Sam Beachy's. Her name is Lizzie" . . . Births — deaths — illness — weddings — folksy happenings such as a carpet ragging — a "frolic" for constructing a hog building — or putting new siding on the barn — these are the items that make up the news the Amish eagerly read.

A copy of the *Budget* is like getting a letter from home. It is the only paper whose big news is in the letters to the editor. With large family ties in all Amish areas, they can follow family news and save personal letter writing.

George Smith, associate editor for the Amish news, carefully reads all letters and prints them as received, except for deleting discussions of doctrinal differences, which are not permitted. Since the paper was first published by John C. Miller, an Amish-Mennonite, in 1890, each editor has accepted the paper's unique relationship with the Amish as a trust.

Two editions are published, National and Home. News of the Sugarcreek area of local interest is added to the news in the national edition; sports, non-Amish social news, local farm sales, and local advertising are included.

The *Budget* is an important stop for Amish visitors to Sugarcreek and their names are published in the paper. On his vacations, associate editor Smith visits with scribes on the way and has developed long-standing friendships with his correspondents. Hopefully, as long as the Amish exist, so will the *Budget*. The circulation of 16,000 copies a week is steadily increasing.

Preference for Farming

"Therefore the Lord God sent him forth from the garden of Eden, to till the soil from whence he was taken."
Genesis 3:23

Worship Services in the Homes

"The Lord of heaven and earth, dwelleth not in temples made with hands."
Acts 17:24

Submission

"Likewise, ye younger, submit yourselves unto the elder. Yea, all of you be subject one to another. . . ."
1 Peter 5:5

Refusal to Bear Arms

". . . whosoever shall smite thee on thy right cheek, turn to him the other also."
Matthew 5:39

"Recompense to no man evil for evil. . . . Live peaceably with all men."
Romans 12:17,18

"For the weapons of our warfare are not carnal, but mighty through God to the pulling down of strong holds."
1 Corinthians 10:4

For Further Reading

Books

Denlinger, Martha A.
Real People: Amish and Mennonites in Lancaster County, Pennsylvania
Herald Press, Scottdale, Pa. 15683, 1975

Hostetler, John A.
Amish Society, Johns Hopkins Press, Baltimore, Md. 21218. Hard-cover
edition revised, 1968; paperback edition, 1970
Amish Life, Herald Press, Scottdale, Pa. 15683, 28th printing, 1975

Hostetler, John A., and Huntington, Gertrude Enders
Children in Amish Society
Socialization and Community Education
Holt, Rhinehart and Winston, Inc., New York, N.Y. 10017, 1971

Mennonite Encyclopedia, The. Available from Herald Press, Scottdale, Pa.
15683. Four volumes, the last one published in 1959. Contains hundreds
of articles on the Amish by states and counties; also their doctrines and
practices. Accessible in many libraries.

Nisely, Jonas A.
Children's Read, Write, Color Book
Jonas A. Nisely, Route 2, Butler, Ohio 44832. Loose-leaf notebook,
pp. 320. Hand-printed for Amish schools by an Amish schoolteacher.

Schreiber, William I.
Our Amish Neighbors, University of Chicago Press, Chicago, Ill. 60637.

Yoder, Joseph W.
Rosanna of the Amish, Herald Press, Scottdale, Pa. 15683. Hard-cover
edition, 12th printing, 1974; paperback edition, 1973

Newspaper

The Budget, Sugarcreek Publishers, Inc., Sugarcreek, Ohio 44681

Magazines

Family Life
Blackboard Bulletin
Young Companion
Pathway Publishers, Rt. 4, Aylmer, Ontario, Canada N5H 2R3 or Rt. 4,
Lagrange, Ind. 46761. Pathway, owned and operated by Amish pub-
lishers, distributes books for the Amish. If interested, send for a catalog.

Many articles and books have been published on the Amish. A misunder-
standing of Amish life by the author often provides a distorted picture. The
above titles will give you a more accurate insight into the Amish way of life.
Libraries usually list Amish as a subheading under Mennonites.

MEATS

MAIN DISHES

SWEET POTATO AND APPLE CASSEROLE

6 boiled sweet potatoes   ¼ cup butter
½ cup brown sugar   4 apples, pared and sliced
1 teaspoon cinnamon   ½ cup water
1 teaspoon salt

Remove potato skins; cut potatoes in slices. Mix brown sugar, cinnamon and salt. Arrange layer of potatoes in buttered casserole; sprinkle with brown sugar mixture and dot with butter. Add layer of apples; sprinkle with brown sugar mixture and dot with butter. Repeat layers, ending with potatoes; pour water over top. Cover casserole. Bake at 400 degrees for 30 minutes or until apples are tender. Uncover; bake until browned. 6 servings.

POOR MAN'S STEAK

Mix:

1 cup club cracker crumbs   1 cup cold water

Let set 2 minutes. Add: 3 pounds ground beef, salt and pepper. Let set several hours. Make patties and roll in flour. Brown on both sides. Pour 1 can cream of mushroom soup (with a little milk added) over the patties. Bake 1 hour at 300 degrees.

BOILED DINNER

4- to 5- pound corned beef brisket   6 medium carrots, peeled
6 small beets, unpeeled   8 medium potatoes, peeled
6 small white turnips, unpeeled   1 small cabbage, quartered
vinegar   prepared mustard

Wash beef and put in large kettle. Cover with cold water. Bring to boil, cover and simmer 4 to 4½ hours, or until tender. Remove meat from kettle. Put beets in saucepan and add some of the broth from the corned beef. Cover and simmer until tender. Add turnips, carrots and potatoes to broth in kettle. Cover and simmer 20 minutes, or until tender. Add cabbage and simmer 15 minutes longer. Remove vegetables and keep hot. Put meat back in broth a few minutes to reheat. Slip skins off beets. Slice beef and arrange in center of hot platter. Surround with the vegetables. Serve with vinegar and mustard. Makes 6 servings with meat left over.

SHIPWRECK

1 pound ground beef
kidney beans
½ cup leftover cooked rice

potatoes
onion (optional)
1 large can tomato sauce

Brown ground beef. Layer in greased casserole dish the browned meat, sliced potatoes (partially cooked or raw), kidney beans, sliced onion rings (if desired). Repeat with second layer of each, then sprinkle rice over top, then add tomato sauce. Bake at 350 degrees about one hour. Serves 8 - 10.

PORCUPINE MEATBALLS

1½ pounds ground beef
½ cup uncooked rice
1 teaspoon salt
½ cup water

¼ teaspoon pepper
¼ cup chopped onion
1 can tomato soup

Combine meat, rice, salt, pepper, and onion. Shape into small balls. Blend soup and water. Put in casserole and pour soup and water over the meatballs. Bake 1 hour at 350 degrees.

SOUR CREAM FRANKFURTERS

8 frankfurters
2 tablespoons margarine
2 tablespoons flour

3 tablespoons catsup
1 cup sour cream
½ teaspoon salt

Cut frankfurters in ½" pieces and brown lightly in hot margarine. Blend in flour. Add ketchup, sour cream and salt. Heat, but do not boil. Makes 4 servings.

SKILLET POT ROAST WITH VEGETABLES

3 to 4 pounds beef for pot roast
    (bottom or top round, eye or
    chuck)
2 tablespoons fat
salt and pepper
onion salt

small new potatoes
carrots
¾ pound whole green beans
summer squash
green onions
½ cup water

In 12" skillet, brown meat in hot fat on all sides. Sprinkle with salt, pepper and onion salt. Add water, cover tightly and simmer about 2½ hours. adding more water if necessary. Add potatoes and carrots (allowing 2 of each per serving.) Cook 30 minutes. Add green beans, squash and green onions. (For each serving, allow 1 small squash and 2 green onions.) Cover; simmer about 30 minutes. Makes 4 servings with meat left over.

YUMZETTI

1 pound hamburger
1 can cream of celery soup
1 can cream of mushroom soup

1 can tomato paste
1 package wide noodles
6 - 8 slices of Velveeta cheese

   Brown hamburg. Cook noodles until tender. Mix together soups and tomato paste. Put in layers in casserole. Bake at 350 degrees for 45 minutes, then remove and add cheese on top. Return to oven until cheese has melted.

BARBECUED HAMBURGER

2 pounds hamburger
1 onion
½ cup catsup
2 tablespoons brown sugar

2 tablespoons mustard
1 teaspoon Worcestershire sauce
1 teaspoon salt

   Make patties, cover with sauce. Simmer about 20 minutes and serve with hamburger buns.

MEAT LOAF

1½ pounds hamburger
onion
garlic salt
pepper

2-4 slices wet bread
green peppers
salt
1 can tomato sauce
2 eggs

   Mix, mold into loaf, place in pan. Bake at 325 degrees to 335 degrees for 1-1½ hours.

STEWED TOMATOES

4 large or 6 medium tomatoes
1 teaspoon salt
one-eighth teaspoon pepper

1 to 2 tablespoons butter or margarine
margarine
sugar to taste

   Peel tomatoes and cut in chunks. Put in saucepan and heat, stirring until juice comes out of tomatoes. Cook, uncovered, 15 to 20 minutes, or until of desired consistency, stirring occasionally. Add salt, pepper, butter, and sugar to taste. Makes about 3½ cups, or 4 to 6 servings.

FOOLPROOF MEAT LOAF

1 pound ground beef or hamburger
1 piece of bread crumbled fine
½ green pepper, finely minced

1 egg
½ onion, finely minced
½ cup catsup

Mix together, shape in loaf, place in pan. Pour more catsup on top. Bake at 325 degrees, for 1½ hours.

GOLDEN FRIED CHICKEN

Wash and dry a 3-pound cut-up broiler-fryer. In paper bag, combine ½ cup all-purpose flour, 1½ teaspoons salt, ¼ teaspoon pepper. Shake the chicken, a few pieces at a time, in flour mixture. In skillet, melt shortening to measure ¼ inch. In a single layer, brown chicken on both sides, removing as it browns. Pour off all but 2 tablespoons fat from skillet. Reduce heat. Cook chicken, covered, 45 minutes. Cook, uncovered, 15 minutes. Serves 4.

AMISH DRESSING

2 quart bread crumbled
¼ cup cooked, diced carrots
½ cup celery, finely cut
3 eggs, beaten

1 cup cooked diced potatoes, salted
1 chicken finely cut
¼ cup parsley, finely cut
2 cups milk

Brown bread in butter in skillet, turn often. Beat eggs, add milk, salt, and pepper and mix together. Put ¼ cup batter in baking pan, brown. Pour dressing in. Bake at 350 degrees to 375 degrees until brown all around.

DUTCH POTATOES

Cook potatoes with the jackets and then slice thin by hand. Put butter or oleo (½ stick) in the skillet. Melt. Add potatoes and sprinkle with flour and then add milk, enough to thicken. Fry slowly so milk doesn't scorch. Season with salt and pepper to taste. Add a few slices of cheese about the last 4 to 5 minutes to melt over the potatoes. Turn very carefully. Serve at once.

OYSTER CASSEROLE

1 package saltine crackers
1 pint oysters
1 stick butter
1 teaspoon salt

½ teaspoon pepper
2 eggs
1 to 2 cups milk

Crumble layer of crackers into 1-quart greased casserole; cover with layer of oysters. Dot with butter and add salt and pepper. Repeat layers until all oysters and crackers are used. Beat eggs with milk; pour over oysters. Bake at 250 degrees for 30 to 35 minutes or until set. Makes 4 servings.

CREAM OF OYSTER SOUP

¼ cup butter
2 tablespoons flour
1 quart milk
1 teaspoon salt

¼ teaspoon celery salt
dash of pepper
½ pint oysters

Melt butter in saucepan over low heat; blend in flour until smooth. Add milk gradually; cook, stirring constantly, until sauce boils and thickens. Add seasonings. Chop oysters; add with oyster liquor to hot mixture. Heat thoroughly until oysters curl. Serve hot with crisp crackers or buttered toast strips. 6 servings.

MUSHROOMS BAKED IN FOIL

Dip 12 large mushrooms in olive or salad oil, or rub or brush with oil. Arrange in one layer on large piece of heavy foil and sprinkle with seasoning salt and pepper. Add other seasonings, if desired. Bring ends of foil together and seal tightly. Bake at 350 degrees for 15 to 20 minutes. Makes 4 servings.

QUICK CORNED BEEF AND CABBAGE

6 small white onions, peeled
salt
6 potatoes scrubbed and halved
1 medium head cabbage, cored and
    quartered

salt and pepper
1 can (12-ounce) corned beef, cut
    in chunks
chopped parsley
prepared mustard

Cook onions in small amount of boiling salted water for 15 minutes. Add potatoes and cook 15 minutes. Add cabbage and cook until vegetables are tender. Season with salt and pepper. Add beef, cover and heat. Sprinkle with parsley and serve with mustard. Makes 6 servings.

CABBAGE-SOUR-CREAM SKILLET

1 small head cabbage
3 tablespoons butter or margarine
salt to taste
dash of nutmeg

1 egg
1 cup sour cream
2 tablespoons sugar
2 tablespoons vinegar

Separate cabbage leaves from head, wash and dry. Shred very fine. Melt butter in skillet; add cabbage, salt and nutmeg and light fry until tender, but not brown. Mix egg with remaining ingredients, pour over cabbage in skillet and heat thoroughly. Makes 4 servings.

BROCCOLI CASSEROLE

¼ cup chopped onion
6 tablespoons butter
2 teaspoons flour
½ cup water
3 eggs, well-beaten

1 8-ounce jar Cheese Whiz
2 packages chopped broccoli,
    thawed and squeezed (to remove
    water)
cracker crumbs

Fry onion in 4 tablespoons butter, add flour and water. When thick, add cheese. Combine sauce with broccoli, add eggs. Pour in greased casserole and top with buttered crumbs, using the remaining 2 tablespoons of butter. Bake 45 to 50 minutes at 350 degrees.

LIMA BEANS WITH SOUR CREAM

1 pound large dried lima beans
2 teaspoons salt
one-third cup margarine
1 cup dark corn syrup

1 teaspoon salt
1 medium onion, chopped
1 teaspoon dry mustard
1 cup sour cream

Soak beans overnight in at least 2½ quarts water with 1 teaspoon salt. Drain and rinse with hot water; drain well. Melt margarine in large saucepan; stir in corn syrup and remaining salt. Add beans. Cover; boil gently for 50 to 60 minutes or until beans are tender. Stir in onion, mustard and sour cream. Turn into 2½-quart casserole; cover. Bake in 350-degree oven for 1 hour. 6 servings.

COTTAGE CHEESE BURGERS

1 pound ground beef chuck
1 cup (8 ounces) cream cottage cheese
¼ teaspoon pepper

1 small onion, minced
1 teaspoon salt

Mix all ingredients and shape in 4 patties. Broil under medium heat 7 minutes on each side, or until of desired doneness. Serve plain or on toasted sandwich rolls.

CHEESE PIE

4 eggs, slightly beaten
1½ cup milk
1-8 ounce wedge natural cheddar
    cheese, shredded

¼ teaspoon salt
dash of pepper
¾ cup cooked diced ham
unbaked pie shell

Combine ingredients for filling and mix well. Pour into pie shell. Bake at 350 degrees for 40 to 45 minutes. Trim with parsley.

DUTCH POTATO PANCAKES

4 or 5 large potatoes
2 eggs

2 tablespoons flour
salt to taste

Grate potatoes, add eggs, well beaten, and other ingredients in order. Stir. Have skillet or griddle greased with bacon drippings. Dip by spoonfuls and flatten slightly. Brown on both sides and serve.

SPICED CABBAGE

1 tart apple
6 cups shredded cabbage
3 tablespoons butter
6 whole cloves
2½ teaspoons salt

¼ teaspoon pepper
½ teaspoon celery salt
one-third cup water
2 tablespoons sugar
¼ cup vinegar

Chop peeled apple coarsely; combine with other ingredients; place in greased, deep 2-quart casserole. Cook, covered, in 350-degree oven one hour. Makes 4 servings.

PANCAKE BURGER BASH

1½ pounds ground beef
1 teaspoon salt
1 can (8 oz.) tomato sauce
1 can (1 lb.) whole kernel corn

one-third cup chopped onion
2-3 teaspoons chili powder
1 can (1 lb.) tomatoes

In Dutch oven or skillet, brown ground beef and onion; drain. Stir in salt, chili powder, tomato sauce, tomatoes and corn (with liquid). Simmer 10 minutes, stir occasionally.

Dumplings:

1½ cups pancake mix
1 egg
½ cup water

½ cup crushed corn chips
2 tablespoons cooking oil

To measure pancake mix, lightly spoon into cup; level. In bowl combine pancake mix with corn chips. Add egg, oil, water; mix well. Spoon batter over bubbling meat mixture. Cover; simmer 15 minutes without removing lid. Dumplings will be puffy and dry on top. Serves 4-6.

HAM & BEAN SOUP

¼ cup oleo

4 tablespoons flour

Heat and stir until golden brown. Add 2 cans soup beans and 2½ cups milk. Brown 1½ cups ham bits in skillet. Add a little water to get a good brown broth. Add to soup. Salt and simmer for 15 minutes.

WIGGLES

1½ pounds hamburger
5 slices bacon
2 small onions
1½ cups diced potatoes
1½ cups diced carrots
1½ cups diced celery

1 can mushroom soup
1 cup peas
1 quart tomato soup
2 pounds Velveeta cheese
1 pound spaghetti

Cook vegetables separately. Fry bacon, take out of skillet. Fry hamburger and onions in grease. Put in a roaster, add potatoes, celery, carrots, and peas. Add mushroom soup and cooked spaghetti. Arrange bacon slices on top. Add grated cheese. Pour tomato soup over top. Bake 1 to 1½ hours at 350 degrees.

OLD-FASHIONED CABBAGE AND POTATO SOUP

1 medium onion, minced
2 tablespoons butter or margarine
3 cups shredded cabbage
¼ cup chopped cabbage
3 cups water

1 teaspoon salt
2 cups diced potato
1 can (14½ ounces) evaporated
  milk
minced parsley
dash of paprika

Cook onion slowly in the butter until golden. Add cabbage to the onion with the water, salt and potato. Cook until tender, 15 to 20 minutes. Add milk and reheat, but do not boil. Serve sprinkled with minced parsley and a dash of paprika. Makes 6 servings.

STRAWBERRY HOT CAKES

2 cups cake mix
½ cup water
one-third cup chopped nuts
whipped cream

1 egg
one-third cup flour
sweetened strawberries

Combine cake mix, egg, and water; beat until smooth. Stir in flour and nuts. Preheat grill. Drop from tablespoons onto lightly greased surface. Cook on both sides until done. Spoon strawberries over hot cakes; top with whipped cream. Serve immediately. Serves 6-8.

BAKED MACARONI AND CHEESE

1 package (8 ounce) elbow macaroni
¼ cup butter or margarine
¼ cup all-purpose flour
8 ounce cheddar cheese, grated (2 cups)

1 teaspoon salt
one-eighth teaspoon pepper
2 cups milk

Preheat oven to 375. Cook macaroni as the package label directs; drain. Meanwhile, melt butter in a medium saucepan; remove from heat. Stir in the flour, salt, and pepper until smooth. Gradually stir in milk. Bring to boiling, stirring. Reduce heat, and simmer mixture one minute. Remove from heat. Stir in 1½ cups cheese and macaroni. Pour into a 1½ quart casserole, and sprinkle remaining cheese over top. Bake 15 to 20 minutes, or until cheese is golden-brown. Makes 4 to 6 servings.

BLUEBERRY PANCAKES

1 cup sifted flour
1 tablespoon sugar
¼ teaspoon cinnamon
1 egg, separated
¾ cup drained blueberries

1½ teaspoons baking powder
½ teaspoon salt
2 tablespoons melted butter
¾ cup milk

Sift flour, baking powder, sugar, salt and cinnamon together,. Add butter to beaten egg yolk; stir in milk. Add to dry ingredients, mixing just enough to moisten. Fold in stiffly beaten egg white. Add blueberries; mix lightly. Pour batter on hot greased griddle. Bake on both sides until done. Serve with butter. Yield: 8 pancakes.

RAISIN SCRAMBLE TOAST

8 slices day-old raisin bread
butter or margarine
5 eggs

one-third cup half-and-half or milk
1 teaspoon seasoned salt

Toast raisin bread until dry and golden brown. Butter each slice, then cut in small cubes; shake off excess crumbs. Beat eggs lightly with half-and-half and salt. Heat 2 tablespoons butter in large skillet. Add eggs and cook over low heat, stirring occasionally, until creamy and eggs begin to thicken. Add toast cubes. Stir gently just until set, but still moist. Makes 6 servings.

APPLE PANCAKES

2 cups flour
4 teaspoons baking powder
2 cups milk
2 tablespoons melted butter

2 tablespoons sugar
1 teaspoon salt
2 eggs, separated
1 cup grated peeled apple

Combine flour, sugar, baking powder and salt in mixing bowl. Combine milk, well-beaten egg yolks and butter in small bowl; mix well. Add to flour mixture beat until smooth. Stir in apple; fold in beaten egg whites. Grease hot griddle for first pancakes only. Pour batter by ½ cupfuls onto griddle; cook until puffy and bubbly. Turn; brown other side. Serve with syrup.

BAKED BEANS

1 pound navy beans   ½ pound salt pork cooked with beans

Soak 2 hours.

Cook 2½ hours or until tender

1 cup catsup   1 tablespoon salt
1 small onion   ½ cup brown sugar
2 tablespoons prepared mustard

Bake 400 degrees for 1 hour.

BAKED MUSHROOMS IN CREAM

8-12 large, fresh mushrooms   ¼ teaspoon pepper
12 drops onion juice   1 tablespoon butter
½ teaspoon salt   ½ cup light cream

Wipe mushrooms with damp cloth; remove stems, reserving for soup or
sauce. Put 1 drop onion juice in each cap; arrange mushrooms, cap side
down, in glass baking dish. Add seasonings. Dot with butter; pour
cream over. Cover; bake at 400 degrees for 15 minutes, or until mushrooms
are tender. Serve on hot toast or over broiled hamburgers. Serves 4.

LEMON CHICKEN

3-pound broiler-fryer, cut up   one-third fresh lemon juice
1 tablespoon butter or margarine   salt and pepper

Preheat oven to 375 degrees, wash chicken; pat dry with paper towels.
Arrange in shallow roasting pan. Dot with butter; sprinkle with ½ teaspoon
salt and dash of pepper. Bake, uncovered, one hour. In small bowl, combine
lemon juice, ½ teaspoon salt, and dash pepper. Pour over chicken; bake 15
minutes longer, or until tender. To serve: Arrange chicken pieces on heated
platter. Spoon pan drippings over them. Trim with thin lemon slices and
parsley sprigs, if desired. Makes 4 servings.

FRIED GREEN TOMATO SLICES

4 medium green tomatoes
1 teaspoon salt
1 teaspoon sugar
½ cup salad oil

½ cup unsifted all-purpose flour
2 eggs
1 cup packaged dry seasoned
   bread crumbs

Trim thin slice from top and bottom of tomato. Cut tomatoes into ½-inch slices on large sheet of waxed paper. Combine flour with ½ teaspoon salt. In small bowl, beat eggs with ½ teaspoon salt and sugar. Dip tomato slices into flour mixture, coating completely. Dip into egg mixture, then into bread crumbs. coating completely. Heat ½ cup salad oil, add tomato slices, saute on each side about three minutes, or until nicely browned. Add more oil as needed. Serve with mustard, if desired.

POTATO SOUP

2 medium-sized potatoes
1 medium-sized onion
butter

1 quart milk
salt and pepper to taste

Peel and cut potatoes in small cubes. Boil potatoes and onion in salt water until almost done. Add milk and bring to boil, then add butter and salt to suit taste. Serve with crackers.

COMPANY CASSEROLE

2 pounds ground beef
2 8-ounce cans tomato sauce
8 ounce cream cheese at room
   temperature
1 tablespoon chopped green peppers
salt and pepper

1 tablespoon butter
1 cup cottage cheese
¼ cup sour cream
one-third cup chopped spring onions
1 eight-ounce box flat noodles

Brown crumbled ground beef in 1 tablespoon butter. Remove from heat stir in tomato sauce and salt and pepper to tast. Combine chopped onions and peppers with cheeses and sour cream. (Green peppers can be omitted if desired.) Cook noodles 7-8 minutes in boiling, generously salted water; drain and rinse quickly once in cold water. In a large, well-buttered casserole spread half of the noodles; cover with cheese mixture plus salt and pepper as desired. Add rest of noodles, dot with 2 tablespoons butter, and then cover with meat misture. Bake at 350 degrees 20-30 minutes, uncovered.

HOT MUSHROOM SANDWICHES

½ pound mushrooms, finely chopped
1 tablespoon minced onion
butter
½ teaspoon salt

dash of pepper
2 tablespoons chopped dill pickle
1 tablespoon mayonnaise
6 thin slices bread, brushed on both
   sides with butter

Saute mushrooms and onion in 3 tablespoons butter until lightly browned. Add seasonings and pickle. Mix with mayonnaise and spread on bread. Assemble 3 sandwiches, cut each in 3 strips and toast under broiler. Makes 9 sandwich strips.

GERMAN NOODLE CASSEROLE

1 pound noodles
1 pound cottage cheese
3 cups sour cream

salt and pepper to taste
butter
milk

Cook noodles; drain. Arrange layers of noodles, cottage cheese and sour cream in baking dish. Season each layer; dot with butter. Pour enough milk over mixture in baking dish to moisten well. Bake at 350 degrees for 45 minutes or until milk is absorbed. 6 - 8 servings.

HOT SHOTS

1 pound cooked ham
½ pound cheese
4 tablespoons mayonnaise

2 tablespoons minced onions
1 cup ripe olives (optional)
1 cup tomato paste

Grind all together, spread on wiener buns and wrap in foil and heat in oven 15 minutes at 350 degrees.

SMOTHERED MUSHROOMS AND CHICKEN LIVERS

¾ pound chicken livers
3 tablespoons flour
3 tablespoons butter or margarine
3 tablespoons minced onion
1½ cups sliced mushrooms

salt
dash of pepper
1 cup chicken broth
¼ cup heavy cream

Sprinkle livers with flour and brown on all sides in the butter. Add onion, mushrooms, ½ teaspoon salt and the pepper. Cook a few minutes, then add broth and simmer 10 minutes. Add cream to livers, heat. Makes 6 servings.

CREAM OF CABBAGE SOUP

1 small head cabbage
2 cups boiling water
2 tablespoons butter or margarine
1 tablespoon minced onion

2 tablespoons flour
1 teaspoon salt
one-eighth teaspoon pepper
dash of nutmeg
2 cups milk, scalded

Shred cabbage very fine. Add boiling water and cook until cabbage is tender, 12 to 15 minutes. Force cabbage through food chopper and put back in liquid. Melt butter, add onion and simmer 3 minutes. Blend in flour, salt, pepper and nutmeg. Add milk and cabbage mixture gradually, stirring. Reheat, taste for seasoning and serve hot. Serves 6.

MUSHROOM SOUP

½ pound mushrooms
4 cups rich chicken broth
2 tablespoons each butter and flour
½ teaspoon salt

dash of cracked pepper
¼ teaspoon ginger
½ cup light cream (optional)
chopped parsley

Remove stems from mushrooms and chop fine. Add to chicken broth, bring to boil and simmer, covered, 20 minutes. Thinly slice caps and saute' in the butter in saucepan 2 to 3 minutes. Blend in flour and seasonings. Gradually stir in stock and mushrooms and cook, stirring, until slightly thickened. Add cream, if desired, and sprinkle with parsley. Makes 1 quart.

CREAM OF MUSHROOM SOUP

½ pound mushrooms, thinly sliced
2 slices onion
3 tablespoons flour
Salt and pepper

3 chicken bouillon cubes
¼ cup butter or margarine
3 cups milk
chopped parsley

Put mushrooms in kettle with 2 cups boiling water, the bouillon cubes and onion. Bring to boil and simmer, covered, 20 minutes. Melt butter in saucepan and blend in flour. Gradually add milk and cook, stirring, until slightly thickened. Add to mushrooms and season to taste with salt and pepper. Sprinkle with parsley. Makes about 1½ quarts.

CALICO BAKED BEANS

2 cans (1 pound each) pork and beans
    with tomato sauce
dash of garlic salt
2 tablespoons brown sugar
½ cup sliced cucumber

½ cup chopped green pepper
½ cup sliced green onion
2 teaspoons minced fresh or
    dried dill
2 pimientos, chopped

    Combine all ingredients and put in 1½ quart casserole. Bake in moderate oven (350 degrees) for 30 minutes. Serves 4 to 6.

POTATO DUMPLINGS

3 cups hot, riced potato, lightly
    packed
1 tablespoon butter
2 eggs, beaten

½ cup fine, dry bread crumbs
1½ teaspoons salt
Dash nutmeg or little grated onion
½ cup flour

    Mix all ingredients well. Form into 1½" balls; roll in a little additional flour. Drop into gently boiling, salted water, soup or stew; cook, uncovered, 5 minutes. Makes 4 to 6 servings.

BEST BAKED BEANS

They bake six to eight hours in seasoned molasses.

1 pound dried pea beans
6 cups water
½ to ¾ pound salt pork
1 medium onion, sliced
1 tart apple, peeled and quartered
½ cup tomato pulp
1 teaspoon worcestershire sauce

½ cup dark molasses
1½ cups meat broth
2 teaspoons salt
½ teaspoon pepper
½ teaspoon celery salt
1 teaspoon dry mustard

    Cover washed beans with water, bring to boil and boil 2 minutes. Cover and let stand one hour. Bring again to boil and cook, covered, until tender; drain. Arrange 2 thin slices each pork and onion in bottom of bean pot. Pour in half the beans. Add apple and pour in remaining beans. Cut remaining pork to the rind in ½" squares and press down into beans, leaving rind exposed. Mix remaining ingredients and pour over beans. Cover and bake at 300 degrees for 6 to 8 hours, removing cover during last hour. Add a little water if necessary. Serves 8.

FRANKS-FAMILY-STYLE

½ cup chopped onion
2 tablespoons butter
1 can Campbells Cheddar Cheese Soup
one-third cup water

4 cups cooked potatoes, sliced
salt
pepper
8 wieners, slashed diagonally

In saucepan, cook onion in butter until tender. Stir in soup and water. In shallow baking dish (10 x 6 x 2) alternate potatoes (sprinkled with salt and pepper) with soup mixture. Top with wieners. Bake at 350 degrees for 30 minutes,

SHEPHERD'S PIE

1 small onion, chopped
2 tablespoons butter
1½ cups diced cooked meat
½ cup diced cooked carrots
1 cup leftover roast gravy

¼ teaspoon salt
dash of pepper
1 cup hot mashed potatoes
grated cheese to taste

Lightly fry onion in butter until brown. Add meat, carrots, gravy and seasonings. Mix together; pour into greased baking dish. Cover with mashed potatoes. Top with grated cheese. Bake at 400 degrees for 15 to 20 minutes or until golden brown. 6 servings.

OLD-FASHIONED BAKED BEANS

2 pounds pea beans or great
    northern beans
1½ to 2 cups unsulphured molasses
2 teaspoons dry mustard
2 cups light brown sugar

3 quarts water
1 medium onion, peeled
1½ teaspoons salt
2 tablespoons instant minced onion
4 to 5 slices bacon

Place beans in large kettle; add water. Bring to boil; boil for 5 minutes. Cover, let stand for one hour. Return to a boil; cover. Reduce heat; simmer for 2 hours and 30 minutes or until beans are tender. Drain beans, reserving 1 cup liquid. Place whole onion in bean pot. Mix beans, molasses, salt, mustard and minced onion; spoon half the bean mixture into pot. Pour in half the reserved liquid; sprinkle with half the brown sugar. Add half the bacon; repeat layers. Bake for about 6 hours at 275 degrees. 20 servings.

BREADS

INDEX FOR BREADS

SOUR CREAM CORN BREAD

¾ cup yellow corn meal
1 cup unsifted all-purpose flour
¼ cup sugar
¼ cup sugar
2 teaspoons double-acting baking
    powder

½ teaspoon soda
¾ teaspoon salt
1 cup sour cream
¼ cup milk
1 egg, beaten
2 tablespoons shortening, melted

Mix all ingredients just enough to blend. Pour into greased 8" square pan and bake at 425 degrees for about 20 minutes.

CARROT BREAD LOAF

1 cup sugar
½ teaspoon baking soda
½ cup vegetable oil
¼ teaspoon cinnamon

1½ cups flour
1 cup grated carrots
2 teaspoons baking powder
2 eggs
½ cup chopped nuts

Mix all dry ingredients together. Add carrots, nuts, oil, and eggs and mix well. Place mixture in a greased or oiled loaf pan and bake for 35-60 minutes in a 350 degree oven.

LEMON NUT BREAD

½ cup shortening
2 eggs
2 teaspoons baking powder
½ cup chopped walnuts

two-thirds cup sugar
2¼ cups sifted flour
½ teaspoons freshly grated lemon peel

Thoroughly cream together shortening and sugar. Add eggs, one at a time, beating well after each addition. Sift together flour, baking powder and salt; add to creamed mixture in three additions, alternately with milk. Beat until smooth after each addition. Stir in lemon peel and walnuts. Spoon into 9 x 5 x 3" loaf pan. Bake at 350 degrees for about one hour, or until done. Pour a lemon glaze over hot bread; let stand 20 minutes before turning out onto rack. Cool completely before slicing.

WHITE BREAD

1 package yeast
½ cup warm water
1¾ cup scalded milk
2 tablespoons sugar

2 teaspoons salt
2 tablespoons cooking oil
5 to 6 cups flour

Dissolve yeast in warm water. Combine milk, sugar, salt and oil; cool to lukewarm. Stir in yeast, mixing well. Add flour gradually; knead. Cover; let rise till doubled in bulk. Punch dough down; let rise again. Shape in 2 loaves; place in greased loaf pans. Let rise till doubled in bulk. Bake for 25 to 30 minutes at 350 degrees.

BAKED DOUGHNUTS

5 tablespoons butter, creamed
1 egg
2¼ teaspoons baking powder
¼ teaspoon nutmeg

½ cup sugar
1½ cups flour
¼ teaspoon salt
½ cup milk

Mix butter, sugar, and egg together; add dry ingredients and milk alternately. Blend well; fill buttered muffin tins ½ full. Bake at 425 degrees for 20 to 25 minutes. Remove from tins; pour glaze over muffins.

SPICY APPLE BREAD PUDDING

1¼ cups applesauce
½ cup cooking oil
3 tablespoons milk
1 teaspoon baking soda
¼ teaspoon salt
¼ teaspoon allspice
¼ cup chopped pecans
½ teaspoon cinnamon

1 cup granulated sugar
2 eggs
2 cups sifted all-purpose flour
½ teaspoon cinnamon
¼ teaspoon nutmeg
½ cup chopped pecans
¼ cup brown sugar
½ teaspoon baking powder

In mixer bowl, thoroughly combine applesauce, the granulated sugar, the oil, eggs, and milk. Sift together flour, soda, baking powder, the first ½ teaspoon cinnamon, the salt, nutmeg, and allspice. Stir into applesauce mixture; beat well. Fold in the ½ cup pecans; turn into well-greased 9 x 5 x 3" loaf pan. Combine the ¼ cup pecans, the brown sugar, and the remaining ½ teaspoon cinnamon; sprinkle over batter. Bake at 350 degrees for one hour or till done. Remove from pan; cool on rack.

CINNAMON ROLLS

½ cup shortening
2 cups scalded milk
2 eggs, beaten
1 teaspoon salt
sugar
1 cup mashed potatoes
2 cakes yeast

¼ cup lukewarm water
7 cups flour
1 cup raisins
1 cup chopped nuts
butter
cinnamon

Dissolve shortening in hot milk; cool. Stir in eggs, salt, 1 cup sugar and potatoes. Dissolve yeast in lukewarm water; add to potato mixture. Stir in flour, raisins and nuts; mix thoroughly. Let rise until doubled in bulk. Roll out ½-inch thick; spread with soft butter. Sprinkle with sugar and cinnamon. Roll and cut; place in well-greased baking pan. Let rise until light. Bake at 350 degrees until golden. Makes 5 dozen rolls.

SUGARPLUM RING

This rich, caramel ring breaks into separate sugarplums.

1 package active dry yeast or 1 cake
  compressed yeast
¼ cup water
½ cup milk, scalded
one-third cup sugar
one-third cup shortening
1 teaspoon salt

3¾ to 4 cups sifted all-purpose flour
2 beaten eggs
¼ cup butter or margarine, melted
¾ cup sugar
1 teaspoon cinnamon
½ cup whole blanched almonds
½ cup candied whole red cherries
one-third cup dark corn syrup

Soften active dry yeast in warm water (110 degrees) or compressed yeast in lukewarm water (85 degrees). Combine scalded milk, the one-third cup sugar, the shortening, and salt; cool to lukewarm. Stir in 1 cup of the flour; beat well. Add softened yeast and eggs. Add remaining flour, or enough to make a soft dough. Mix thoroughly and place in a greased bowl, turning once to grease surface. Cover and let rise till double, about 2 hours. Punch down and let rest 10 minutes. Divide dough into 4 parts. Cut each part into 10 pieces and shape into balls. Dip balls in the melted butter, then in the ¾ cup sugar blended with the cinnamon. Arrange one-third of the balls in well-greased 10-inch tube pan. Sprinkle with some of the almonds and cherries. Repeat with two more layers. Mix corn syrup with butter left from dipping balls; drizzle over top. Cover and let rise in warm place till double, about 1 hour. Bake at 350 degrees for 35 minutes. Cool 5 minutes; invert pan and remove ring.

ICEBOX ROLLS

2 packages yeast
½ cup lukewarm water
2 eggs
two-thirds cup sugar
2 teaspoons salt

¾ cup shortening
1 cup mashed potatoes
1 cup scalded milk, cooled
6 cups sifted flour

Dissolve yeast in lukewarm water. Place eggs, sugar, salt and shortening in large bowl; beat well. Add potatoes, milk and yeast mixture; beat until blended. Work in flour, by hand, one cup at a time, to make stiff dough. Place dough in greased bowl; turn dough to grease well. Cover; let rise for 2½ hours or until light and doubled in bulk. Work dough down; shape into rolls with floured hands. Place in greased pan; cover and let rise again until doubled in bulk. Bake for 15 minutes at 400 degrees.

DATE OATMEAL BREAD

1½ cups milk
1 cup oatmeal
1 cup pitted dates, sliced
2 cups flour

4 teaspoons baking powder
1½ teaspoons salt
¾ cup sugar
1 egg

Scald milk; add oats and dates. Cool. Sift flour, baking powder, salt and sugar together. Beat egg and add to cooled milk mixture, add sifted dry ingredients and mix well. Place in buttered loaf pan and bake at 325 degrees for 1 hour. Makes one loaf.

APRICOT WHEAT BREAD

1½ cups dried apricots, finely cut
1(8½-ounce) can crushed pineapple
1 cup light brown sugar, firmly
     packed
½ cup butter or margarine
2 cups sifted all-purpose flour
2 teaspoons baking powder

½ teaspoon salt
5 Nabisco shredded wheat biscuits,
     crumbled (about 2 cups)
¾ cup chopped walnuts
2 eggs, well beaten
¾ cup milk

In a saucepan, simmer apricots, pineapple and ¼ cup brown sugar covered for 10 minutes, stirring occasionally. Remove from heat. Add butter or margarine and stir to melt. Cool to room temperature. Sift flour, baking powder and salt. Add remaining brown sugar, shredded wheat biscuit crumbs and nuts. Mix well. Stir in eggs, milk and apricot mixture. Blend thoroughly. Turn into a greased 9 x 5 x 3" loaf pan. Bake at 350 degrees for one to 1¼ hours. Turn out on rack to cool. Makes 1 loaf.

BANANA OATMEAL BREAD

2 cups biscuit mix
1 cup oatmeal
¼ teaspoon soda
¾ teaspoon baking powder
¾ cup brown sugar, packed

½ cup chopped walnuts
½ cup golden raisins
1 egg
½ cup milk
2½ ripe bananas, mashed

Combine biscuit mix, oatmeal, soda, baking powder, sugar, nuts, and raisins in large bowl and mix well. Beat egg and mix with milk and bananas. Add to flour mixture and stir just to blend. Turn batter into greased 9 x 5" loaf pan and bake at 350 degrees for 50 to 55 minutes. Cool on rack before slicing.

GUM DROP WALNUT BREAD

½ cup sugar
1 egg
1 cup chopped walnuts

1¼ cups milk
3 cups biscuit mix
1 cup chopped gum drops (do not use black)

Heat oven to 350 degrees. Mix sugar, milk, eggs, and the biscuit mix. Beat hard for a half minute. Stir in walnuts and gum drops. Pour into well greased 9 x 5 x 3" loaf pan. Bake 40 to 50 minutes, until toothpick thrust in center comes out clean. Crack in top is typical. Cool before slicing. To store, foil-wrap

PINEAPPLE-DATE LOAF

¼ cup soft butter or margarine
½ cup sugar
1 egg
¼ teaspoon lemon extract
1 (8½ oz.) can crushed pineapple
¼ cup chopped nuts
2½ cups sifted all-purpose flour

2½ teaspoons baking powder
¼ teaspoon baking soda
1 teaspoon salt
½ cup finely chopped, pitted dates
¼ cup water
¼ cup chopped maraschino cherries, well drained

Cream butter and sugar; add egg and lemon extract. Drain pineapple, reserving liquid. Add crushed pineapple and nuts to creamed mixture. Sift dry ingredients together. Add dates and mix well, separating date pieces with your fingers. Stir dry ingredients into creamed mixture alternately with reserved pineapple juice plus ½ cup water. Fold in the chopped maraschino cherries. Pour into a greased 9 x 5 x 3 "loaf pan. Bake at 375 degrees about 55 minutes. Cool in pan 10 minutes. Remove; cool completely. Makes 1 loaf.

APRICOT-NUT BREAD

2½ cups sifted flour
2 teaspoons salt
¼ cup shortening
1 cup diced dried apricots
1 cup milk

1 cup sugar
3 teaspoons baking powder
½ cup chopped nuts
2 eggs, well beaten
cream cheese, softened

Sift flour, sugar, salt and baking powder together; cut in shortening until mixture resembles coarse meal. Add nuts and apricots. Combine eggs and milk; add to dry ingredients, stirring until just dampened. Spoon batter into greased loaf pan. Bake for one hour at 350 degrees. Spread with cream cheese.

BISCUITS

2 cups sifted all-purpose flour
1 teaspoon salt
two-thirds to ¾ cup milk

1 tablespoon baking powder
¼ cup shortening

Sift flour, baking powder and salt together; cut in shortening until mixture is crumbly. Add enough milk to make a soft dough. Turn out on lightly floured board; knead for 30 seconds. Roll dough out to ½ inch thick; cut with floured biscuit cutter. Place on ungreased baking sheet. Bake at 450 degrees for 10 to 12 minutes or until lightly browned. Makes 12 biscuits.

SALT RISING BREAD

1 cup milk
1½ teaspoons salt
1 cup lukewarm water
5¼ cups sifted flour

2 tablespoons sugar
¼ cup white corn meal
2 tablespoons melted shortening

Scald milk; remove from heat and stir in 1 tablespoon sugar, salt and corn meal. Turn into 2 quart jar or pitcher, cover and set in pan of water hot to the hand. Let stand in warm place for 6 hours, or until it ferments. Then stir in rest of lukewarm water, remaining 1 tablespoon sugar, shortening, and 2 cups flour. Beat thoroughly. Put 2 quart jar full back into pan of hot water and let rise until sponge is full of bubbles. Pour into mixing bowl. Stir in remaining cups of flour. Shape into loaves. Put in greased pans. Brush with melted fat. Let raise until two and a half times size, and bake in 250 degrees oven 35 to 40 minutes.

SOUR CREAM MUFFINS

1 egg
1 cup sour cream
2 tablespoons butter, melted
2 cups sifted all-purpose flour

¼ cup sugar
2 teaspoons baking powder
½ teaspoon soda
½ teaspoon salt
¼ cup milk

Beat egg and sour cream until light. Add butter, sifted dry ingredients and milk. Stir only until dry ingredients are dampened. Fill 12 greased 2¾" muffin cups half full with batter. Bake at 400 degrees about 20 minutes. Makes 12.

LEMON MUFFINS

2 cups self-rising flour
2 tablespoons sugar
1 + one-third cups milk

1 box lemon pudding mix
¼ cup oil
confectioners' sugar

Sift flour, pudding mix and sugar together in mixing bowl. Combine oil and milk; blend into flour mixture all at once. Stir only until moistened. Fill greased muffin cups two-thirds full. Bake at 425 degrees for 20 to 25 minutes. Sprinkle with confectioners' sugar. Makes 1½ dozen.

DATE NUT BREAD

1½ cups snipped dates (about ½ pound)
1 teaspoon soda
1 cup boiling water
1 egg, beaten
1 cup sugar

2 cups sifted flour
1 teaspoon baking powder
½ teaspoon salt
1 cup chopped walnuts

Sprinkle dates with soda; stir in boiling water. Let stand until cool. Meanwhile, in large bowl thoroughly combine beaten egg and sugar. Sift together dry ingredients and add all at once along with date mixture. Mix thoroughly, beating until well blended. Stir in walnuts. Spoon into 9 x 5 x 3" loaf pan. Bake at 325 degrees about 1 hour, or until done. Turn out onto wire rack to cool thoroughly before slicing.

PEANUT BUTTER BREAD

2 cups all-purpose flour
½ teaspoon salt
½ cup peanut butter
1 cup milk
½ cup chopped salted peanuts

3 teaspoons baking powder
½ cup sugar
2 well-beaten eggs
1 teaspoon grated lemon rind
melted butter

Sift dry ingredients together; rub in peanut butter until mixture is crumbly. Combine eggs, milk, and lemon rind; add to flour mixture. Pour into greased 9 x 5 loaf pan; sprinkle with peanuts. Bake for 50 to 60 minutes at 325 to 350 degrees. Brush hot bread with melted butter. Let set overnight; remove from pan and slice.

QUICK NUT BREAD

2 cups sifted flour
3 teaspoons baking powder
½ teaspoon salt
½ cup brown sugar

1 cup milk
1 egg, beaten
2 tablespoons melted shortening
1 cup chopped pecans

Sift flour, baking powder, salt and brown sugar together. Combine milk, egg, shortening and pecans; add to dry ingredients, mixing well. Pour into greased loaf pan. Bake in 350 degree oven for 1 hour or until lightly browned. Makes 1 loaf.

SUGARED YEAST DOUGHNUTS

1 cup milk
1 envelope yeast
3½ cups sifted flour
¼ cup shortening

1 teaspoon salt
¼ cup sugar
1 egg
shortening

Heat milk slightly; dissolve yeast. Add 1½ cups flour; beat until smooth. Cover; let rise in warm place for about 2 hours, until doubled in bulk. Cream shortening, salt and sugar together; add egg, blending well. Stir into yeast sponge; add remaining flour. Beat well for 5 minutes by hand. Rub top with shortening; let rise again until doubled in bulk. Roll out ½-inch thick; cut with floured doughnut cutter. Allow to rise for 45 minutes. Fry for about 3 to 5 minutes in deep 365 degree shortening until brown. Drain; sprinkle with additional sugar. Makes 2 dozen doughnuts.

CAKES

COOKIES

PORK CAKE

Pour:

1 cup boiling water over: 1 lb. fat pork, ground

Add:

1 lb. seeded raisins   1 tablespoon nutmeg
2 cups sugar   1 tablespoon cloves
1 cup molasses   ½ teaspoon salt
2 tablespoons cinnamon   2½ cups flour

   Bake in slow oven until done. This cake can be wrapped in foil and kept in refrigerator for months.

COOKIE SHEET CAKE

Mix in bowl:

2 cups flour
2 cups sugar   ½ teaspoon salt

Melt and bring to boil:

2 sticks butter
1 cup water   3 tablespoons cocoa

Beat:

2 eggs
1 teaspoon vanilla   ½ cup buttermilk

   Add to above. Pour into a well greased cookie sheet and bake at 350 degrees for 20 minutes.

Frosting for Cookie Sheet Cake:

Melt:
1 stick butter
3 tablespoons cocoa   6 tablespoons milk

Add:
1 box powdered sugar
1 teaspoon vanilla   ½ cup pecans

   Ice cake while warm. (Cool about 10 minutes before icing.)

71

HICKORY NUT CAKE

2 cups sugar
½ cup butter
1 cup milk
2½ cups flour

2 teaspoons baking powder
1 cup nuts
pinch of salt
3 eggs

Cream sugar and butter. Add eggs. Beat well. Then add flour with baking powder and milk alternately. Fold in nuts. Bake at 350 degrees for 30 minutes.

NUT ICING

1½ cups sugar
1 cup sweet cream

½ cup hickory nuts
lump of butter
1 teaspoon vanilla

Boil sugar and cream together until almost done. Then add: ground nuts, lump of butter and 1 teaspoon vanilla

COFFEE CAKE

Cream together:

1 cup oleo

1¼ cups sugar
2 eggs

Then add:

1 cup sour cream

1 teaspoon vanilla

Mix:

2¼ cups flour
1 teaspoon baking powder

½ teaspoon soda

Add to the mixture above.

Topping

¾ cup chopped nuts
2 teaspoons cinnamon

2 tablespoons sugar

Mix this well in separate container. Put ½ of above dough in greased and floured pan. Add ½ of topping over it, spread evenly. Add the rest of dough and remainder of topping layers. Cut through with knife. Bake at 350 degrees 45 to 50 minutes.

SOUR CREAM MOLASSES SQUARES

1 cup butter
½ cup sugar
1 cup light molasses
1 egg
3½ cups sifted cake flour
1 teaspoon soda

1 teaspoon each cinnamon and ginger
¾ teaspoon salt
½ cup sour cream
frosting
chopped nuts

Cream butter and sugar until light. Beat in molasses and egg. Add sifted dry ingredients and sour cream and beat until smooth. Spread in greased 15" x 10" x 1" baking pan. Bake at 350 degrees about 30 minutes. Cool in pan. Then spread with frosting and sprinkle with nuts, pressing down into frosting. Cut in 35 squares.

FROSTING

In heavy saucepan, mix 1 cup dairy sour cream, 2 cups sugar and dash salt. Put over high heat and cook rapidly, stirring vigorously, about 10 minutes or until small amount of mixture forms a soft ball when dropped in very cold water. Remove from heat, add ½ teaspoon vanilla and beat until smooth and creamy. Spread quickly.

RED VELVET CAKE

½ cup shortening
2 eggs
1 teaspoon vanilla
1 teaspoon salt
2½ cups cake flour
1½ cups sugar

2 oz. red food coloring
2 tablespoons cocoa
1 cup buttermilk
1 teaspoon soda
1 teaspoon vinegar

Cream shortening, sugar and vanilla. Add eggs, one at a time, beating well. Make paste of food coloring and cocoa and add to above. Sift flour and salt and add alternately with milk. Beat well. Combine vinegar and soda and add at once. Beat well. Bake at 350 degrees for 30 minutes.

Icing for Red Velvet Cake:

5 tablespoons flour
1 cup milk
1 cup powdered sugar

1 teaspoon vanilla
1 cup butter

Cook flour and milk together and then cover and let cool. Cream sugar and butter well. Add vanilla. When flour mixture is cooled, add it to the sugar and butter and beat well.

DATE BROWNIE CAKE

1 cup pitted dates
¾ cup sugar
½ cup butter or margarine
1 tablespoon grated lemon rind
1 package (6 ounces) semi-sweet
   chocolate pieces

2 eggs
1¼ cups sifted all-purpose flour
¾ teaspoon baking soda
½ teaspoon salt
1 cup coarsely chopped nuts

Cook first 4 ingredients and ½ cup water until sugar is dissolved and dates are softened, stirring. Remove from heat, beat in chocolate. Cool slightly and beat in eggs, one at a time. Add sifted dry ingredients alternately with 1 cup water, beating until smooth. Pour into 13" x 9" x 2" pan lined on bottom with waxed paper. Sprinkle with nuts. Bake in moderate oven 350 degrees about 35 minutes.

APPLESAUCE-DATE CAKE

2 cups unsifted all-purpose flour
2 teaspoons baking soda
1 teaspoon cinnamon
½ teaspoon allspice
½ teaspoon nutmeg
¼ teaspoon cloves
¼ teaspoon salt
2 eggs

1 cup light-brown sugar, firmly
   packed
½ cup soft butter or margarine
2 cups hot applesauce
1 cup chopped dates
¾ cup coarsely chopped walnuts

Preheat oven to 350 degrees. Grease well and flour a 9 x 9 x 2 inch baking pan. Into large bowl, sift flour with baking soda, cinnamon, allspice, nutmeg, cloves, and salt. Then add the eggs, brown sugar, soft butter, and 1 cup hot applesauce; beat until the ingredients are combined. Beat 2 minutes longer. Add remaining applesauce, dates, and walnuts; beat 1 minute. Pour batter into prepared pan. Bake 50 minutes, or until cake tester inserted in center comes out clean. Let cool in pan 10 minutes. Remove from pan, and let cool on wire rack. Frost top of cooled cake with Cream-Cheese Frosting. Makes 9 servings.

Cream-Cheese Frosting for Applesauce-Date Cake

1 package (3 oz.) cream cheese, softened
1 tablespoon soft butter or margarine

1 teaspoon vanilla extract
2 cups sifted confectioners' sugar

In small bowl combine cream cheese, butter, and vanilla; beat until smooth and fluffy. Gradually add confectioner' sugar; continue beating until fluffy.

CHOCOLATE CUPCAKES

3 squares unsweetened chocolate
¼ cup soft butter or margarine
1 cup granulated sugar
2 eggs
1 teaspoon vanilla extract
confectioners' sugar frosting

1¾ cups sifted all-purpose flour
1 teaspoon baking powder
½ teaspoon each soda and salt
two-thirds cup buttermilk
1¼ cups rolled oats
chopped nuts

Melt and cool chocolate, cream butter and sugar. Add eggs, one at a time, beating thoroughly after each addition. Add chocolate and vanilla; blend. Add sifted dry ingredients and buttermilk; beat until smooth. Stir in oats. Fill 2" paper baking cups two-thirds full of batter. Bake on cookie sheet at 375 degrees for 10 to 15 minutes. Cool, frost and decorate with nuts. Makes about 36 chocolate cupcakes.

AMISH CAKE

1 stick oleo
1 pound brown sugar
2 cups buttermilk or sour milk

3 cups flour
2 teaspoons soda (put in milk)

Cream together sugar, oleo, add buttermilk, soda, add flour and vanilla. Bake at 375 degrees till done. Take out and spread topping on, put in oven until bubbly, about 10 minutes. Topping: 6 tablespoons soft butter, 4 tablespoons milk, 1 cup brown sugar, ½ cup nuts or more if desired.

DATE-WALNUT SQUARES WITH WHIPPED CREAM

¾ cup finely chopped dates
two-thirds cup chopped walnuts
3 tablespoons flour
1 teaspoon baking powder
2 eggs, separated

1 teaspoon vanilla extract
¼ teaspoon salt
½ cup light-brown sugar, firmly
   packed
½ cup heavy cream, whipped

Preheat oven to 350 degrees. Lightly grease an 8 x 8 x 2" baking pan. Place dates and walnuts in a large bowl. Sift flour and baking powder over them. Toss dates and walnuts to mix well. Add slightly beaten egg yolks and the vanilla; mix well. In medium bowl, beat egg whites and salt until soft peaks form. Add sugar gradually, beating until stiff peaks form. With rubber scraper, fold into date-walnut mixture just until combined. Turn into prepared pan; bake 20 minutes. Let cool in pan 10 minutes. Cut into 9 squares. Serve warm, with whipped cream. Makes 9 servings.

EASY CHOCOLATE ROLL-UP

¼ cup butter
1 cup chopped pecans

1 and one-third cups flaked coconut
1 can (15½ oz.) sweetened condensed
  milk

CAKE:

3 eggs
1 cup sugar
one-third cup cocoa
two-thirds cup all-purpose flour

¼ teaspoon salt
¼ teaspoon baking soda
one-third cup water
1 teaspoon vanilla   .

Oven 375 degrees. 1 Cake Roll - 8 to 10 servings. Line 15 x 10" jelly roll
pan with foil. Melt butter in pan, sprinkle nuts and coconut evenly in pan;
drizzle with condensed milk.
In mixer bowl, beat eggs at high speed 2 minutes until fluffy. Gradually add
sugar; continue beating 2 minutes. No need to sift flour; spoon into cup, level.
Add remaining ingredients; blend 1 minute at low speed. Pour evenly into pan.
Bake at 375 degrees for 20 - 25 minutes until cake springs back when touched in
center. Sprinkle cake (in pan) with powdered sugar. Cover with towel. Place
cookie sheet over towel; invert. Remove pan and foil. Start with 10" side, roll
up jelly-roll fashion using towel to roll cake.

JAM CAKE

2 cups sugar
4 cups flour
½ cup butter or more (can use 1 cup)
2 cups blackberry jam
1 cup black walnuts or more (can
    use any other nuts)
1 cup raisins or more

2 teaspoons cinnamon
2 teaspoons cloves
2 teaspoons nutmeg
2 teaspoons allspice
2 teaspoons soda dissolved
1 cup buttermilk
6 eggs or more

Place all ingredients in large pan and mix thoroughly. Bake in layers at
300 degrees for about an hour. 1½ times this recipe makes 2 large cakes.

Icing for Jam Cake:

2 cups sugar
1 cup sweet milk   ½ cup butter

Cook until about as thick as cream. Have icing cooked and ready to put on
cake as soon as cake is done. Pour on while icing and cake both are hot.

DUTCH APPLE CAKE

1 cup all-purpose flour
1½ teaspoons baking powder
¼ teaspoon salt
¼ cup seedless raisins
sugar
butter or margarine

1 egg, well beaten
¼ cup milk
3 cups peeled tart-apple wedges, ¼"
   thick
½ teaspoon cinnamon
¼ teaspoon nutmeg

Mix first 4 ingredients and 2 tablespoons sugar. Cut in one-third cup butter. Add combined egg and milk and blend well. Spread in greased 10 x 6 x 2 inch glass baking dish. Arrange apple wedges in rows in batter, pressing straight edges down slightly. Brush with 2 tablespoons melted butter and sprinkle with mixture of spices and 2 tablespoons sugar. Bake at 400 degrees for 30 to 40 minutes. Cut in squares and serve warm.

SWEET CHOCOLATE CAKE

1 package sweet cooking chocolate
½ cup boiling water
1 cup butter or margarine
2 cups sugar
4 eggs, separated

1 teaspoon vanilla
½ teaspoon salt
1 teaspoon soda
2½ cups sifted cake flour
1 cup buttermilk

Melt chocolate in boiling water; cool. Cream butter and sugar until fluffy; beat in egg yolks, one at a time. Add chocolate and vanilla; mix well. Sift salt, soda and flour together; add flour mixture to chocolate mixture alternately with buttermilk, beating until smooth. Fold in stiffly beaten egg whites; pour in three 8-inch waxed-paper-lined cake pans. Bake in 350-degree oven for 30 to 40 minutes. Cool layers; spread with Coconut-Pecan Frosting. Stack layers; do not frost sides.

Coconut-Pecan Frosting

1 cup evaporated milk
1 cup sugar
3 eggs yolks, beaten
2 tablespoons margarine

1 teaspoon vanilla
1 and one-third flaked coconut
1 cup chopped pecans

Mix milk, sugar, egg yolks, margarine and vanilla in saucepan. Cook, stirring over medium heat for 12 minutes or until thickened. Add coconut and pecans; beat until thick enough to spread. Makes 15 servings.

CRAZY CHOCOLATE CAKE

1½ cups flour
1 cup white sugar
1 teaspoon soda
½ teaspoon salt
1 teaspoon vanilla

3 tablespoons cocoa
one-third cup salad oil
1 tablespoon vinegar
1 cup milk

Sift dry ingredients together onto a sheet of waxed paper. Sift again into an ungreased 8" square cake pan. Make 3 little "wells" in the dry ingredients. Pour the salad oil into the first, vinegar into the second, and vanilla into the third. Add the milk and stir with a fork until mixture is well blended. Bake for 30 minutes at 350 degrees.

PINEAPPLE NUT CAKE

2 cups all-purpose flour
2 cups sugar

2 teaspoons soda
½ teaspoon nutmeg

Sift together. Fold in one at a time: 1 large can crushed pineapple (drained), 2 eggs, ½ cup chopped nuts, ¾ cup cooked and drained raisins. Then bake at 325 degrees 35 to 45 minutes.

PRUNE-SPICE CAKE

1½ cups sifted all-purpose flour
¾ cup granulated white sugar
¼ cup brown sugar
1 teaspoon baking powder
½ teaspoon baking soda
½ teaspoon ground cinnamon
¼ teaspoon ground ginger

¼ teaspoon salt
½ cup cooking oil
1 4¾-ounce jar (½ cup) strained
  prunes
1 egg
1 teaspoon vanilla
½ cup chopped walnuts

In bowl, sift together first 8 ingredients. Add the oil, ½ cup cold water, the prunes, egg, and vanilla. Blend, then beat 1 minute. Turn batter into a greased and floured 9 x 9 x 2" baking pan. Sprinkle nuts atop batter. Bake in 350 degrees oven for 30 minutes; cool in pan. Combine ½ cup sifted confectioners' sugar, one-eighth teaspoon ground cinnamon, and 1 tablespoon light cream. Drizzle over cake.

TEXAS SHEET CAKE

Sift together:

2 cups sugar   2 cups flour

Boil together:

1 stick oleo   1 cup water
4 tablespoons cocoa

Pour this over sugar and flour. Mix slightly, then add 2 eggs, 1 teaspoon soda dissolved in ½ cup of buttermilk, 1 teaspoon vanilla. Mix, bake at 350 degrees for 20 minutes. While cake is baking, make frosting: 1 stick oleo, 6 tablespoons milk, 4 tablespoons cocoa. Boil together, then add 1 box powdered sugar, 1 teaspoon vanilla, and stir. Frost cake while hot.

SNOWBALL CAKE

2 packages plain gelatin   1 tablespoon lemon juice
1 No. 2 can crushed pineapple   2 packages Dream Whip
¾ cup sugar   1 large angel food cake
½ teaspoon salt

Dissolve gelatin in 4 tablespoons cold water. Add 1 cup boiling water. Add crushed pineapple and lemon juice, also salt and sugar. Mix well and chill. When partially congealed, beat 1 package of Dream Whip and fold in. Break up cake in small pieces, put in bowl lined with Saran Wrap. Put in layers of cake pieces, then mixture, until all is used up, with cake on top. Chill overnight, then turn out on a plate, remove Saran Wrap, and frost with other package of Dream Whip.

COFFEE-RAISIN SPICE CAKE

1 cup coffee   1 teaspoon cinnamon
1 cup granulated sugar or packed   1 teaspoon nutmeg
    brown sugar (best with brown)   ½ teaspoon salt
1½ cups raisins, chopped   ½ teaspoon baking powder
one-third cup butter, margarine   1 teaspoon baking soda
    or other shortening   2 cups all-purpose flour
½ teaspoon ground cloves

Put first 7 ingredients in saucepan, bring to boil and boil 3 minutes; cool thoroughly. Add remaining ingredients, and mix well. Put in 9" x 5" x 3" loaf pan lined on bottom with waxed paper and bake at 275 degrees for 1 hour and 10 minutes, or until done. Turn out on rack and peel off paper. Turn right side up. Serve plain or top with thin lemon confectioners' sugar frosting.

MY FAVORITE APPLE SAUCE CAKE

No icing is needed for this moist cake.

2 eggs
1½ cups sugar
1 cup butter
2 teaspoons vanilla
3 cups applesauce
2 cups chopped walnuts
4 cups raisins

1 cup chopped dates
3½ cups sifted flour
4 teaspoons soda
2 teaspoons cinnamon
2 teaspoons cloves
½ teaspoon nutmeg
½ teaspoon ginger

Mix eggs, sugar, vanilla, and butter. Blend well and set aside. In another bowl, sift flour, salt, soda, and spices. To this add raisins, nuts and dates and mix well. Add applesauce to first mixture, then add in the flour mixture. Mix well and pour into a greased tube pan. Bake in 325 degree oven for one and ¾ hours or until done. Use a cake tester or broom straw to test cake for doneness. If a less spicy taste is desired, you may cut down on cloves and other spices.

POKE AND POUR CAKE

1 package white cake mix
2 egg whites
1½ cups water
1 package (3 oz.) cherry, strawberry, or
    raspberry Jello

1 cup boiling water
1 cup cold water

Prepare cake mix following package directions with egg whites and 1½ cups water. Pour into generously greased and lightly floured 13 x 9-inch pan. Bake according to package directions. Cool 15 minutes. Meanwhile, prepare Jello, following package directions. With tines of fork, poke holes to bottom of cake at ½ inch intervals. Gently pour Jello evenly over cake. Refrigerate 3 to 4 hours before serving. Serve with whipped cream, if desired.

PRUNE CUPCAKES

½ cup butter or margarine
1 cup sugar
1 teaspoon vanilla extract
2 eggs
1 cup pitted, cooked prunes
1½ cups sifted flour

1½ teaspoons baking powder
½ teaspoon salt
1 teaspoon cinnamon
¼ teaspoon cloves
½ cup milk
½ cup chopped nuts

Cream butter; gradually add sugar, and cream until light. Add vanilla, and eggs, one at a time, beating well after each. Fold in prunes. Add sifted dry ingredients alternately with milk, beating well. Add nuts. Half-fill greased 2½" muffin pans; bake in 375-degree oven for 20 minutes. Makes 21.

SOUR CREAM POUND CAKE

3 cups flour
¼ teaspoon soda
one-eighth teaspoon salt
2 sticks butter
3 cups sugar
6 eggs, separated

1 teaspoon vanilla flavoring
1 teaspoon lemon or almond flavoring
1 cup sour cream
¾ cup powdered sugar
juice of 1 lemon

Sift flour, soda and salt together. Cream butter and sugar; beat in egg yolks one at a time. Stir in flavorings; beat in flour mixture alternately with sour cream. Fold in beaten egg whites. Place batter in greased tube pan. Bake at 300 degrees for one hour and 30 minutes or at 350 degrees for one hour and 15 minutes. Cool cake in pan for 10 minutes; turn onto rack. Blend powdered sugar and lemon juice; drizzle over hot cake.

GREAT-GRANDMA'S SHEEP-WAGON CARROT CAKE

The following recipe from Pennsylvania has the wonderful name of "Great Grandma's Sheep-Wagon Carrot Cake" (why or how the recipe got its name, we do not know, but we would love to hear the story).

GREAT GRANDMA'S SHEEP-WAGON CARROT CAKE

Put in a middle-sized saucepan:

1 and one-third cups sugar
1 and one-third cups water
1 cup raisins
1 tablespoon butter

2 large finely grated carrots
1 teaspoon cinnamon
1 teaspoon cloves
1 teaspoon nutmeg

Simmer these ingredients for five minutes and then cover and rest them for 12 hours. (Why they get so tired is a mystery, but if you don't rest them, the mixture loses something in taste.) Then add:

1 cup chopped walnuts
2½ cups sifted flour
½ teaspoon salt

1 teaspoon soda
2 teaspoon baking powder

Bake in two oiled loaf pans for 2 hours at 275 degrees. Cool and then foil-wrap. This is good served warm.

RHUBARB COFFEE CAKE

2 cups flour
1½ cups brown sugar
½ cup butter
1 egg
1 cup buttermilk

½ teaspoon soda
½ teaspoon salt
1½ teaspoons vanilla
1½ cups rhubarb, cut up

Cream sugar and butter. Add egg alternately and sifted dry ingredients with buttermilk and vanilla. Stir in fruit. Pour into 9 x 9 square pan. Sprinkle on top:

1 cup white sugar, mixed with
    Bake 40 minutes at 350 degrees.

1 teaspoon cinnamon

APPLE CRUMB CAKE

butter or margarine
1 cup fine dry bread crumbs
1 cup graham-cracker crumbs
2 tablespoons granulated sugar

1 teaspoon cinnamon
2 cups applesauce
confectioners' sugar
vanilla sauce

Melt ½ cup butter in skillet. Add next 4 ingredients and stir until well blended and golden brown. In greased 8" layer-cake pan, put layers of crumbs and applesauce, beginning and ending with crumbs. Dot top layer with 2 tablespoons butter. Bake at 375 degrees for 25 to 30 minutes. Cool on rack. Turn out of pan, sprinkle top with confectioners' sugar and serve with vanilla sauce. Makes 6 servings.

VANILLA SAUCE

1 egg
2 tablespoons sugar
2 teaspoons cornstarch

2 cups milk
2 teaspoons vanilla extract

In medium bowl, beat well egg, sugar and cornstarch. Bring milk to boil and gradually pour over egg mixture, beating constantly. Pour mixture back into saucepan and bring to boil, stirring. Remove from heat and add vanilla. Chill, beating occasionally. Makes 2 cups.

GRAHAM CRACKER CAKE

2 cups sugar
1 package graham cracker crumbs
5 eggs
1 teaspoon vanilla
1 cup milk

1 cup coconut
1 cup butter
2 teaspoons baking powder
1 cup crushed pineapple (well drained)
1 cup chopped English walnuts

Cream butter and sugar, add eggs and beat. Add cracker crumbs, baking powder and beat. Then add all other ingredients and beat. Bake at 350 degrees for 35 to 45 minutes.

MAHOGANY CAKE

1½ cups sugar
two-thirds cup butter
1¼ cups milk
½ cup cocoa

1 teaspoon vanilla
1 teaspoon soda
2 scant cups of flour
3 eggs

Cream sugar and butter. Add well-beaten eggs. Take one-half of the milk, add to the cocoa and cook until the consistency of custard, then cool and add to the butter, sugar, and egg, then add to the other half of milk with the teaspoon full of soda dissolved in milk. Lastly add flour, vanilla and beat. Bake in moderate oven.

WACKY CHOCOLATE CAKE

Sift together in large bowl:

1½ cups flour
2 heaping tablespoons cocoa
¼ teaspoon salt

1 teaspoon soda
1 cup sugar

Make a hole in the center and pour in:

½ cup Mazola oil
1 teaspoon vanilla

1 cup warm water

Beat thoroughly. Bake in a large pan, 40 minutes at 350 degrees, or until done. This makes one layer and is very moist. It keeps well.

PEANUT BUTTER APPLE CAKE

¼ cup soft butter
½ cup peanut butter
1 cup sugar
1 egg
1¼ cups sifted all-purpose flour
1 teaspoon soda

1 teaspoon salt
½ teaspoon cinnamon
¼ teaspoon nutmeg
¼ teaspoon ground cloves
1 cup canned applesauce

Cream butter, peanut butter and sugar. Add egg and beat well. Sift dry ingredients and add alternately with applesauce to first mixture, stirring until smooth. Pour into 8" x 8" x 2" pan, lined on the bottom with waxed paper. Bake at 350 degrees for 40 minutes, or until done. Cool 5 to 10 minutes. Turn out on rack; peel off paper. Cool well.

RHUBARB CAKE

1½ cup brown sugar
1 stick oleo
1 egg
½ teaspoon salt
1½ to 2 cups diced rhubarb

2 cups flour
1 cup buttermilk
1 teaspoon soda
vanilla

Topping:

¼ cup white sugar   1 teaspoon cinnamon

Sprinkle on top of unbaked cake. Bake at 375 degrees 35 minutes.

FRUIT COCKTAIL CAKE

2 cups flour
1½ cups sugar
1 teaspoon soda

2 eggs
1 No. 303 can fruit cocktail with
  juice

Mix dry ingredients, add eggs and fruit. Pour into ungreased large cake pan. Mix ¼ cup brown sugar and ½ cup chopped nuts. Sprinkle over cake. Bake at 325 degrees 40-45 minutes.

Topping:

¾ cup sugar   ½ cup evaporated milk
1 stick oleo

Boil 5 minutes. Pour on cake while warm.

NO BAKE COOKIES

Boil together for 1 minute:

½ cup milk
2 cups sugar

3 tablespoons cocoa
1 stick oleo

Remove from heat and add:

½ cup peanut butter
3 cups quick rolled oats

1 teaspoon vanilla

Cool. Stir, then drop on waxed paper.

CARROT COOKIES

1 cup sugar
1 egg
½ cup ground carrots
2 cups sifted flour
½ cup butter

1 teaspoon lemon flavoring
½ cup chopped raisins
2 teaspoons baking powder
½ teaspoon salt

Mix and drop by teaspoon on greased sheet. Bake at 400 degrees for 10-12 minutes. These stay moist.

CRY BABY COOKIES

Mix together:

½ cup each sugar, vegetable shortening, seedless raisins, chopped nuts.

Add:

1 teaspoon baking soda, dissolved in ½ cup strong hot coffee.

Stir together:

2½ cups flour
¼ teaspoon salt

1 teaspoon each cinnamon and ginger

Add to liquid mix. Drop by small teaspoonfuls, at least an inch apart, on greased cookie sheets and bake in moderate hot oven (375 degrees) about 15 minutes, then remove with spatula from tins.

BUSY DAY DROP COOKIES

Cream together:

1 cup shortening   2 cups brown sugar

Then add:

½ cup sour milk   2 eggs, beaten

Sift together and add to batter:

3½ cups flour   1 teaspoon soda
1 teaspoon baking powder   1 teaspoon salt

Blend in 1 cup nuts and 1 teaspoon vanilla. Drop on baking sheet and bake 15 minutes in 350-degree oven.

SUGAR COOKIES

2 cups sugar   1 teaspoon soda
1 cup shortening   4 teaspoons baking powder
2 eggs   1 teaspoon salt
1 cup milk   pinch of cream of tartar
flour

Mix sugar, shortening and eggs together with electric mixer. Add milk; stir in flour to make a soft dough. Add soda, baking powder, salt and cream of tartar; mix well. Refrigerate for one hour. Knead part of the dough at a time on floured board until soft and easy to handle. Cut as desired; place on cookie sheets. Bake at 400 degrees for 10 to 12 minutes. Makes 5 dozen cookies.

SOUR CREAM RAISIN NUT COOKIES

½ cup soft butter or margarine   ½ teaspoon soda
1 cup brown sugar, packed   ½ teaspoon nutmeg
1 egg   ½ cup sour cream
2 cups sifted cake flour   ½ cup seedless raisins
2 teaspoons baking powder   ¾ cup chopped nuts
½ teaspoon salt

Cream butter and sugar until light. Beat in egg. Add sifted dry ingredients alternately with sour cream, beating until smooth. Stir in raisins and nuts. Drop by teaspoonfuls on lightly greased cookie sheets. Bake at 400 degrees for 10 to 12 minutes. Makes about 4 dozen.

CRISP PEANUT BUTTER COOKIES

1 cup margarine or butter
1 cup peanut butter
1 cup sugar
1 cup firmly packed brown sugar
2 eggs, beaten

2½ cups sifted flour
1 teaspoon baking powder
1 teaspoon baking soda
1 teaspoon salt
1 teaspoon vanilla

Stir together margarine, peanut butter and sugars until blended. Beat in eggs and vanilla. Sift together flour, baking powder, baking soda and salt over sugar mixture. Stir until well blended. If necessary, chill dough until it can be easily handled. Shape into 1-inch balls. Place about 2 inches apart on greased baking sheet. Flatten with floured bottom of glass or with floured fork making corsswise pattern. Bake in 350-degree oven 12- to 15 minutes or until lightly browned. Makes 6 dozen cookies.

COCONUT MACAROON COOKIES

1 cup brown sugar
1 cup white sugar
1 cup melted shortening
2 eggs, beaten
1 cup coconut

1 teaspoon vanilla
½ teaspoon salt
1 teaspoon soda
1 cup flour
4 cups rolled oats

Mix ingredients in order given. Shape in small balls. Place on cookie sheet and bake 15 minutes in moderate oven (350 degrees).

THE ULTIMATE BROWNIES

1 package (4 oz.) Baker's German
   Sweet Chocolate
5 tablespoons butter
1 package (3 oz.) cream cheese
1 cup sugar
3 eggs
1 tablespoon all-purpose flour

1½ teaspoons vanilla
½ teaspoon baking powder
¼ teaspoon salt
½ cup unsifted all-purpose flour
½ cup coarsely chopped nuts
¼ teaspoon almond extract

Melt chocolate and 3 tablespoons butter in saucepan over very low heat, stirring constantly; cool. Cream remaining butter with cheese until softened. Gradually add ¼ cup sugar, creaming until fluffy. Blend in 1 egg, 1 tablespoon flour, and ½ teaspoon vanilla. Set aside. Beat 2 eggs until thick and light. Gradually beat in ¾ cup sugar. Add baking powder, salt, and ½ cup flour. Blend in cooled chocolate mixture, nuts, 1 teaspoon vanilla, and the almond extract. Spread half of chocolate batter in greased 8- or 9-inch square pan. Top with cheese mixture. Spoon remaining chocolate batter onto cheese mixture. With spatula, swirl through batter to marble. Bake at 350 degrees for 35 to 40 minutes. Cool; cut into bars. Makes about 20.

SAUCEPAN BROWNIES

one-third cup shortening
2 squares chocolate, unsweetened
½ teaspoon vanilla extract
1 cup sugar

2 eggs
¾ cup sifted all-purpose flour
¼ teaspoon salt
¾ cup chopped nuts

Melt shortening and chocolate in saucepan over low heat, stirring; cool. Beat in vanilla and sugar. Add eggs, one at a time, beating well after each addition. Sift flour and salt; add nuts. Stir into chocolate mixture. Spread in buttered 8" x 8" x 2" pan. Bake at 325 degrees for about 25 minutes. Cool and cut in squares. Makes 16.

SOUR CREAM DROP COOKIES

¼ cup soft butter
1 cup sugar
1 egg
2 cups sifted all-purpose flour
½ teaspoon salt

½ teaspoon soda
1 cup sour cream
cinnamon-sugar mixture

Cream butter and sugar until light. Beat in egg. Add sifted dry ingredients alternately with sour cream and beat until smooth. Drop by rounded teaspoonfuls onto greased cookie sheets. Sprinkle with cinnamon-sugar mixture. Bake at 375 degrees for about 15 minutes. Makes about 5 dozen cookies.

FRUIT COOKIES

1½ cups sugar
½ cup butter
1 egg
2 cups raisins
1 cup nuts

pinch of salt
1 cup hot water in which raisins were
   cooked
2 teaspoons soda dissolved in hot water
3 cups flour
spices to taste

Cream butter and sugar; add egg beaten lightly. Add hot water and soda slowly; then sifted flour. Stir in raisins and nuts and bake in square pan at 375 degrees. Cut in squares. (May use cookie sheet with rim. Don't use nuts, or not so many, when storing. Store between wax or brown paper, otherwise they stick together. May add candied fruit, also, or sprinkle some on top when baking.)

RAISIN TOFFEE BARS

1 cup sifted flour
½ teaspoon salt
½ cup soft butter or margarine
1 cup brown sugar, firmly packed

1 teaspoon vanilla flavoring
2 eggs
1 cup all-bran cereal
1 cup seedless raisins

Sift together flour and salt. Combine butter and sugar in mixing bowl; mix thoroughly. Add vanilla and eggs; beat well. Stir in all-bran and raisins. Add flour mixture; stir until thoroughly combined. Spread in well-greased 9 x 9" pan. Bake at 350 degrees about 30 minutes, or until done. Cool in pan on wire rack. Frost with confectioners' icing; let stand until set. Cut into bars about 3 x 1½". Chopped nutmeats or flaked coconut may be sprinkled over icing, if desired.

CONFECTIONERS' ICING: Combine 1 cup sifted confectioners' sugar, 1 tablespoon soft butter or margarine, ½ teaspoon vanilla flavoring and 1 to 2 tablespoons milk. Beat until smooth; spread evenly over cooled Raisin Toffee Bars. Makes 18 bars.

ROCKY ROAD BARS

Cut 10 marshmallows in quarters. Arrange in buttered 9" x 5" x 3" loaf pan. Fill spaces between marshmallows with ½ cup broken walnut meats. Melt 1 package (8 ounces) semisweet chocolate squares and pour over contents of loaf pan. Cool until firm and cut in 15 bars.

PEANUT BUTTER CRACKLES

1¾ cups sifted flour
1 teaspoon baking soda
½ teaspoon salt
½ cup margarine or butter
½ cup peanut butter
½ cup sugar

½ cup firmly packed brown sugar
1 egg
1 teaspoon vanilla
sugar
chocolate candy kisses or stars

Sift together flour, baking soda and salt. Stir margarine to soften; mix in peanut butter until blended. Gradually add sugars, mixing until creamy and well blended. Beat in egg and vanilla. Stir in flour mixture until well mixed. Shape dough into 1-inch balls. Roll in sugar and place on ungreased baking sheet. Bake in 375-degree oven 12 minutes or until lightly browned. Remove from oven and quickly press chocolate candy firmly into top of each cookie; cookie will crack around the edges. Makes 4 dozen cookies.

PUMPKIN NUT COOKIES

½ cup shortening
1 cup sugar
2 eggs, beaten
1 cup pumpkin
2 cups sifted all-purpose flour
4 teaspoons baking powder

1 teaspoon salt
2½ teaspoons cinnamon
½ teaspoon nutmeg
¼ teaspoon ginger
1 cup raisins
1 cup chopped nuts

Cream shortening; add sugar gradually. Cream until light and fluffy. Add eggs and pumpkin; mix well. Sift flour, baking powder, salt and spices together. Stir in dry ingredients and mix until blended. Add raisins and nuts. Drop by teaspoon - fuls on greased cookie sheets. Bake in 350-degree oven for approximately 15 minutes. Makes 4 dozen cookies.

AMISH CHURCH COOKIES

2 cups brown sugar
3 eggs
1 teaspoon soda

1 cup lard
½ cup milk
2 teaspoons baking powder
3½ cups flour

Add 2 teaspoons vanilla. Add a little more flour if they get too flat. Drop on sheet. Bake (375 degrees).

GERMAN CREAM CHEESE BROWNIES

1 package (4 ounces) Baker's German
    Sweet Chocolate
5 tablespoons butter
1 package (3 ounces) cream cheese
1 cup sugar
3 eggs

½ cup plus 1 tablespoon unsifted
    flour
1½ teaspoons vanilla
½ teaspoon baking powder
¼ teaspoon salt
½ cup coarsely chopped nuts
¼ teaspoon almond extract

Melt chocolate and 3 tablespoons butter over very low heat, stirring constantly. Cool. Cream remaining butter with the cream cheese until softened. Gradually add ¼ cup sugar, creaming until light and fluffy. Stir in 1 egg, 1 tablespoon flour, and ½ teaspoon vanilla until blended. Beat remaining eggs until fluffy and light in color. Gradually add remaining ¾ cup sugar, beating until thickened. Fold in baking powder, salt and remaining ½ cup flour. Blend in cooled chocolate mixture. Stir in nuts, almond extract, and remaining 1 teaspoon vanilla. Measure 1 cup chocolate batter and set aside. Spread remaining chocolate batter in a greased 9-inch square pan. Pour cheese misture over the top. Drop measured chocolate batter from tablespoon onto the cheese mixture; swirl the mixtures together with a spatula just to marble. Bake at 350 degrees for 35 to 40 minutes. Cool. Cut in bars or squares. Cover and store in the refrigerator. Makes about 20 brownies.

PIES

DESSERTS

INDEX FOR PIES AND DESSERTS

CONTINUED ON PAGE 136

ALMOND CRUST-CHERRY CREAM PIE

½ cup chopped silvered almonds
pastry for 1 9-inch pie shell
1½ cups sweetened condensed milk
one-third cup lemon juice
1 teaspoon vanilla
½ teaspoon almond extract

½ cup whipping cream, whipped
two-thirds cup cherry juice
¼ cup sugar
1 tablespoon cornstarch
3 drops of red food coloring
2 cups drained pitted sour cherries

Add chopped almonds to pastry. Roll out on floured surface to fit
9-inch pie pan. Place in pan; prick sides of pie crust. Bake at 425 degrees for
10 to 12 minutes; cool. Combine milk, lemon juice, vanilla and almond
extract; mix until thickened. Fold in whipped cream; spoon into cooled shell.
Blend cherry juice, sugar and cornstarch in saucepan; cook over low heat,
stirring constantly, until thickened and clear. Add red food coloring and
cherries; spread over cream filling. Chill for 2 to 3 hours.

RAISIN CREAM PIE

Use 1 cup raisins, 1½ cups water, two-thirds cup sugar, 1 teaspoon
lemon juice. Cover and simmer for 15 minutes. Dissolve 2 tablespoons cornstarch in ½ cup sweet cream. Add yolks of 2 eggs, add to boiled raisins and
let come to a boil until thickened. Pour into baked pastry shell and cover with
meringue made with the whites of 2 eggs.

PINEAPPLE CHEESE PIE

1 (1-pound 4-ounce) can crushed
    pineapple
sugar
2 tablespoons cornstarch
½ teaspoon salt
1 (8-ounce) package cream cheese

2 eggs
½ cup milk
1 teaspoon vanilla
1 unbaked 9-inch pie shell with
    high rim

Combine undrained pineapple, two-thirds cup sugar, cornstarch and ¼
teaspoon salt. Cook over moderate heat 5 minutes, stirring frequently.
Remove from heat and cool slightly. Soften cheese and blend in ½ cup sugar
and remaining ¼ teaspoon salt. Beat in eggs, one at a time. Blend in milk
and vanilla. Turn pineapple filling into unbaked pie shell and pour cheese
mixture carefully over it. Bake on lowest shelf of hot oven (400 degrees F.)
10 minutes. Reduce heat to moderately slow (325 degrees F.) and bake 40
to 50 minutes longer. Cool thoroughly. Garnish as desired with pastry
circles. Makes 1 (9-inch) pie.

CHERRY PIE

1 cup cherry juice	¼ teaspoon almond extract
two-thirds cup sugar	1 3-oz. package cream cheese
one-eighth teaspoon salt	½ cup powdered sugar
2 tablespoons cornstarch	1 teaspoon vanilla
2 cups pie cherries	1 cup whipping cream
1 tablespoon. butter	1 baked 10-inch pie shell

Combine cherry juice, sugar and salt; bring to a boil. Blend cornstarch with small amount of water; add to sugar mixture. Cook, stirring constantly, until thickened. Add cherries, butter and almond extract. Refrigerate until cool. Mix cream cheese, powdered sugar and vanilla until creamy. Whip cream; fold into cream cheese mixture. Pour creamed mixture into pie shell; top with cherry mixture. Refrigerate.

OATMEAL PIE CRUST

Scald two parts of fine oatmeal with one part of hot water; mix well and roll thin. As this bakes very quickly, fruit which requires much cooking must be cooked first before making the pies. This crust is very tender, possessing all the desirable qualities of the shortening pie crust.

PEACH AND APPLE PIE

Mix:

¾ cup sugar	½ teaspoon grated lemon rind
2 tablespoons flour	¼ teaspoon nutmeg
one-eighth teaspoon salt	½ teaspoon cinnamon
1 tablespoon lemon juice	

Line a 9" pie pan with pastry rolled one-eighth inch thick. Half-fill pan with equal amounts of sliced fresh peaches and apples (about 1½ cups each). Sprinkle with half the sugar mixture. Top with 3 cups more fruit, and remaining sugar mixture. Dot with 1 tablespoon butter. Adjust top crust (lattice, if desired), and bake at 425 degrees for 40 to 50 minutes.

OATMEAL PIE NO. 1

Mix:

1¼ cups white sugar
1¼ cups dark corn syrup
1¼ cups quick-cook oatmeal

3 beaten eggs
1 teaspoon vanilla
1 stick (¼ pound) margarine, melted

Pour into 2 (8in.) unbaked pie shells. Bake at 350 degrees for 35 minutes.

OATMEAL PIE NO. 2

2 beaten eggs
1 cup sugar
1 cup light corn syrup
¾ cup coconut

¾ cup quick-cook oatmeal
½ cup evaporated milk
¼ cup melted butter
1 teaspoon vanilla

Mix all together. Fills 9 in. unbaked shell generously. Bake at 400 degrees for first 10 minutes, then switch to 200 degrees for about another 40 minutes or until filling is set in center.

OATMEAL PIE NO. 3

1 cup brown sugar
two-thirds cup white sugar
3 well beaten eggs
2 tablespoons soft butter

two-thirds cup quick cook oats
two-thirds cup coconut
1 teaspoon vanilla

Bake in 9 in. pie shell at 350 degrees for 35 to 40 minutes or until firm in center.

Oatmeal pies make good picnic fare, being easier to carry. Taste like pecan but much less expensive.

CHOCOLATE CREAM PIE

2 sq. unsweetened chocolate
1½ cups sugar
3 tablespoons cornstarch
½ teaspoon salt
3 cups milk

3 egg yolks, lightly beaten
1 tablespoons butter
1½ teaspoons vanilla
1 9-in. baked pie shell

Shave chocolate into strips. Mix sugar, cornstarch, chocolate and salt in saucepan; stir in milk gradually. Cook over medium heat; stirring constantly, until mixture thickens and boils. Boil for one minute. Remove from heat. Stir half the hot mixture into egg yolks; blend egg yolk mixture into hot mixture remaining in saucepan. Boil for one minute, stirring constantly. Remove from heat. Blend in butter and vanilla; pour immediately into pie shell. Chill pie for 2 hours. Top with whipped cream. One-half cup cocoa may be substituted for chocolate.

PECAN PUMPKIN PIE

Bake at 425 degrees for 15 minutes, then at 375 degrees for 30 minutes. Makes 1 9" pie.

1 pieshell with fluted edge
2 eggs
1 can (1 lb.) pumpkin
½ cup granulated sugar
pecan topping

½ cup firmly packed brown sugar
1½ teaspoons pumpkin-pie spice
1 teaspoon salt
1 tall can evaporated milk

Beat eggs slightly in a large bowl; stir in pumpkin, granulated and brown sugars, pumpkin-pie spice, salt, and evaporated milk. Pour into prepared pastry shell. Bake at 425 degrees for 15 minutes. Lower oven temperature to 375 degrees. Continue baking 20 minutes. Spoon pecan topping around edge on pie. Bake 10 minutes longer, or until custard is almost set but still soft in center. (Do not overbake; custard will set as it cools.) Cool pie completely on a wire rack.

Pecan Topping:

Cream 3 tablespoons butter or margarine with two-thirds cup firmly packed brown sugar in small bowl; stir in two-thirds cup chopped pecans until well blended.

RHUBARB CREAM PIE

2 cups diced rhubarb
2 tablespoons butter
1¼ cups sugar
2 tablespoons cornstarch

¼ cup sweet cream
2 egg yolks, well beaten
one-eighth teaspoon salt
1- 9" baked pie shell

Melt butter, add rhubarb, and 1 cup sugar, cook slowly, stirring constantly until tender. Mix ¼ cup sugar, cornstarch, egg yolks, cream and salt. Add to rhubarb mixture. Cook until thick, about 3 minutes. Cool and pour in pie shell. Top with meringue made of 2 egg whites and 4 tablespoons sugar. Brown in oven.

SHOOFLY PIE

1½ cups flour
½ cup sugar
½ teaspoon nutmeg
1 teaspoon cinnamon
one-eighth teaspoon salt

one-third cup butter or oleo
¾ cup unsulphured molasses
¾ cup water
½ teaspoon soda
1 9" unbaked shell

Sift together flour, sugar, nutmeg, cinnamon and salt. Add butter. Cut in with 2 knives or pastry blender to resemble coarse crumbs. Combine molasses, water and soda. Pour into unbaked pastry shell. Spoon crumbs over top. Bake at 375 degrees for approximately 35 minutes.

OLD-FASHIONED SHOO FLY PIE

For the Juice:

1 cup water
1 cup molasses

1 teaspoon cloves

For the Crumbs:

3 cups flour
1 cup brown sugar
½ cup shortening

1 teaspoon cinnamon
1 teaspoon cream of tartar
1 teaspoon soda

PUMPKIN PIE

(For 2 9-inch pies, double this recipe, pour into 2 pastry shells and bake as directed.)

2 eggs, slightly beaten
1½ cups Libby's pumpkin
¾ cup sugar
½ teaspoon salt
1 teaspoon cinnamon

½ teaspoon ginger
¼ teaspoon cloves
1 and two-thirds cups evaporated milk or light cream
1 9" unbaked pie shell

Mix filling ingredients in order given. Pour into pie shell. Bake in preheated hot oven (425 degrees) for 10 minutes. Reduce temperature to moderate (350 degrees) and continue baking for 45 minutes or until knife inserted into center of pie filling comes out clean.

RHUBARB SPONGE PIE

2 eggs, separated
2 tablespoons flour
2 tablespoons butter or margarine, melted
1 cup milk

1 cup sugar
1 teaspoon lemon juice
2 cups diced fresh rhubarb
unbaked 9" pie shell

Beat egg yolks and stir in flour and butter. Gradually stir in milk. Add sugar and lemon juice and mix well. Add stiffly beaten egg whites. Arrange rhubarb in shell and pour mixture over top. Bake at 450 degrees for 10 minutes. Reduce heat to 350 degrees and bake 40 to 45 minutes longer. Cool before cutting.

OLD-FASHIONED PUMPKIN PIE

3 eggs
1 can (1 lb) pumpkin
½ cup light-brown sugar, packed
½ cup granulated sugar
1 teaspoon cinnamon
½ teaspoon ginger

¼ teaspoon nutmeg
one-eighth teaspoon cloves
½ teaspoon salt
¾ cup milk
½ cup heavy cream
9-inch unbaked pie shell

Preheat oven to 350 degrees. In large bowl, beat eggs slightly. Add pumpkin, sugars, spices, salt; beat until well blended. Slowly add milk and cream. Pour into shell; bake 60 to 70 minutes, or until knife inserted in center comes out clean. Cool on rack. Serve with whipped cream.

GREEN-TOMATO PIE

6 to 8 medium green tomatoes
2 tablespoons lemon juice
1 teaspoon grated lemon or orange rind
½ teaspoon salt
¼ teaspoon cinnamon

¾ cup sugar
2 tablespoons cornstarch
1 tablespoon butter or margarine
pastry for 9" double-crusted pie

Wash tomatoes, peel and slice. Combine with next 4 ingredients in sauce-pan and cook 15 minutes, stirring frequently. Mix sugar and cornstarch. Add to tomato mixture and cook until clear, stirring constantly. Add butter and cool slightly. Line 9" pie pan with pastry and pour in mixture. Cover with pastry, seal edges and cut several gashes to allow steam to escape. Bake at 425 degrees for 40 to 50 minutes. Serve slightly warm or cool.

FLAKY PASTRY

4 cups all-purpose flour
1¾ cups vegetable shortening (not oil)
1 tablespoon sugar

2 teaspoons salt
1 tablespoon vinegar
1 egg

With fork, mix first 4 ingredients. In small bowl, beat ½ cup water and remaining ingredients together. Add to first mixture and blend with fork until dry ingredients are moistened. With hands, mold dough in a ball and chill at least 15 minutes. Makes two double-crust 9" pies and one 9" shell.

SOUR CREAM PIE

1 cup sugar
1 cup water

1 cup raisins

Boil these three ingredients 10 minutes.

Add:

1 cup sour cream
3 teaspoons cornstarch
2 egg yolks, beaten

cinnamon
nutmeg

Cook until thick. Pour into baked crust. Add meringue. This is a very good pie.

APPLE PIE

pastry for 9-inch two-crust pie
¾ to 1 cup sugar
1 teaspoon cinnamon or nutmeg

6 to 7 cups sliced pared apples
1½ tablespoons butter

Heat oven to 425 degrees. Mix sugar and cinnamon; mix lightly through apples. Heap up in pastry-lined pie pan. Dot with butter. Cover with top crust which has slits cut in it. Seal and flute. Cover edge with 2- to 3- inch strip aluminum foil to prevent excessive browning. Bake 50 to 60 minutes or until crust is nicely browned and apples are cooked through (test with fork). Serve warm or cold. If desired, serve with whipped cream, ice cream or slices of cheese.

PEANUT BUTTER-CHIFFON PIE

1 envelope unflavored gelatin
½ cup sugar
¼ teaspoon salt
1 cup milk

2 eggs, separated
two-thirds cup smooth peanut butter
1 cup dairy sour cream
1 baked 9" pie shell

In top part of small double boiler, mix gelatin, ¼ cup of the sugar and the salt. Add milk and egg yolks and beat with rotary beater until blended. Put over simmering water and cook, stirring, until mixture thickens slightly and coats a spoon. Remove from heat, pour into bowl and beat in peanut butter. Cool thoroughly. Beat egg whites until foamy. Gradually add ¼ cup sugar and beat until stiff. Stir sour cream into peanut butter mixture. Then fold in egg whites. Pile lightly into shell and chill until firm. Serve with peanut butter topping or whipped cream.

PEANUT BUTTER TOPPING

½ cup cold milk
½ teaspoon vanilla extract
2 tablespoons peanut butter

2 tablespoons sugar
1 package (2 oz.) dessert topping
   mix

Blend all ingredients in small bowl of electric mixer. Then beat at high speed until topping forms soft peaks. Serve on pies, cakes, or pudding. Makes about 1½ cups.

GERMAN CHOCOLATE CHEESE TARTS

1 8-ounce package cream cheese,
   softened
¼ cup milk
¾ cup sugar
2 squares (2 ounces) unsweetened
   chocolate, melted

2 egg yolks
2 egg whites, stiffly beaten
¼ cup finely chopped pecans
tart-size pastries

Beat cream cheese until fluffy; gradually add milk and sugar and beat well. Beat in melted chocolate and egg yolks. Fold in beaten egg whites. Pour into tart-size crusts and top with chopped pecans. Chill until firm.

BANANA CREAM PIE

3 tablespoons flour
1 tablespoon cornstarch
½ cup sugar
¼ teaspoon salt
1 cup milk

1 cup cream
2 egg yolks, beaten
1 teaspoon vanilla
1 baked 8 or 9-inch pie shell
sliced bananas

Mix dry ingredients in saucepan. Stir milk into cream; stir in egg yolks. Add to dry ingredients. Cook until thick; add vanilla. Cool. Pour into pie shell. Add bananas. Coconut may be substituted for bananas. Add ¼ cup coconut to filling; sprinkle ½ cup coconut on top. Makes 5 servings.

DEEP CHERRY PIE WITH SHORTCAKE CRUST

1 can (19 ounces) red, sour pitted
   cherries
sugar
2 tablespoons flour
dash salt

1 tablespoon lemon juice
1 tablespoon butter
1 cup prepared biscuit mix
¼ cup milk

Drain cherries; heat juice to boiling. Add combined ¾ cup sugar, flour and salt; cook until thickened, stirring constantly. Cool slightly. Add lemon juice, butter and cherries; pour into casserole. Combine biscuit mix and 2 tablespoons sugar; add milk, and beat well. Spoon batter over cherries. Bake at 400 degrees for 20 to 25 minutes, or until brown. Makes 4 servings.

GRATED-CARROT PIE

½ cup packed brown sugar
1 tablespoon flour
¼ teaspoon salt
½ teaspoon cinnamon
2 eggs, slightly beaten
1 cup milk

1 teaspoon lemon juice
1 tablespoon butter, melted
1½ cups lightly packed, finely
    grated peeled raw carrots
    (about 4 medium)
unbaked 8" pie shell

Mix first 4 ingredients. Beat in remaining ingredients. Pour into shell and bake at 400 degrees for 45 minutes or until firm. Serve slightly warm or cold.

CRUSTLESS COCONUT PIE

2 eggs
1 cup sugar
1 cup milk
pinch salt
¼ teaspoon baking powder

¼ cup flour
½ teaspoon vanilla
½ stick butter (melted)
1 cup coconut

Mix all ingredients together. Bake in 8-inch pie pan at 350 degrees for 30 minutes. This pie has no crust.

RHUBARB CUSTARD PIE

3 eggs
3 tablespoons milk
2 cups sugar
¼ cup flour

¾ teaspoon nutmeg
4 cups diced rhubarb
1 unbaked pie shell
butter

Beat eggs lightly; beat in milk, sugar, flour and nutmeg. Stir in rhubarb. Pour filling into pie shell; dot with butter. Bake at 425 degrees for 1 hour or until custard is set.

PECAN PIE

3 eggs, beaten
½ cup sugar
1 cup dark corn syrup
1 cup chopped pecans

¼ cup melted butter
¼ teaspoon salt
1 teaspoon vanilla
1 unbaked pie shell

Mix filling ingredients together. Pour into pie shell. Bake 40 minutes in 350-degree oven, or until filling is set.

APPLE PIE

pastry
1¼ cups sugar
2 tablespoons flour
¾ teaspoon cinnamon
½ teaspoon nutmeg
one-eighth teaspoon salt

6 cups thinly sliced, pared, tart
   cooking apples (about 2 lb)
1½ teaspoons grated lemon peel
1 tablespoon butter
1 egg yolk

    Roll out half of pastry to line a 9-inch pie plate. Chill. Combine sugar, flour, cinnamon, nutmeg, salt; mix well. Add apples; toss lightly. Turn into pie plate, mounding in center. Sprinkle with lemon peel; dot with butter. Roll out rest of pastry for top. Make several slits in center, for steam vents. Fold edge of top crust under bottom crust; press together; crimp. Mix yolk with 1 tablespoon water; brush on crust. Bake at 425 degrees for 40 to 50 minutes, or until apples are tender and crust is golden. Serve warm. Makes 6 to 8 servings.

OATMEAL PIE

3 eggs, slightly beaten
1 cup sugar
1 cup white Karo
1 cup oatmeal

1 tablespoon flour
½ teaspoon salt
1 tablespoon melted butter

    Mlx altogether and add 1 teaspoon vanilla, 1 cup oatmeal last. Put in unbaked pie crust. Bake about 45 minutes.

GERMAN SWEET CHOCOLATE PIE

1 package (4 ounce) Baker's German
   Sweet Chocolate
¼ cup butter
1 and two-thirds cups (14½ oz. can)
   evaporated milk
1½ cups sugar
3 tablespoons cornstarch
one-eighth teaspoon salt

2 eggs
1 teaspoon vanilla
1 unbaked 10-inch pie shell or
   2 unbaked 8-inch pie shells
1 and one-third cups Baker's
   Angel Flake Coconut
½ cup chopped pecans

    Melt chocolate with butter over low heat, stirring until blended. Remove from heat; gradually blend in milk. Mix sugar, cornstarch, and salt thoroughly. Beat in eggs and vanilla. Gradually blend in chocolate mixture. Pour into pie shell. Combine coconut and nuts; sprinkle over filling. Bake at 375 degrees for 45 minutes. Filling will be soft, but will set while cooling. Cool at least 4 hours before cutting.

WALNUT-COFFEE PIE

½ cup brown sugar
½ cup soft butter
1 cup sugar
3 eggs
¼ teaspoon salt

¼ cup heavy cream
½ cup strong coffee
1½ cups chopped walnuts
1 teaspoon vanilla
1 unbaked 9-in. pie shell

Cream brown sugar and butter. Add sugar and mix well. Add eggs, one at a time, beating well after each addition. Add salt, cream and coffee. Cook over boiling water, stirring for 5 minutes. Remove from heat; stir in 1 cup walnuts and vanilla. Pour into pie shell. Bake at 350 degrees for 1 hour. Sprinkle remaining walnuts on top. Bake for 5 minutes longer.

PUDDING PECAN PIE

1 package vanilla pudding and pie
    filling
1 cup corn syrup
¾ cup evaporated milk

1 egg, slightly beaten
1 cup chopped pecans
1 unbaked 8-inch pie shell

Blend pudding mix with corn syrup. Gradually add evaporated milk and egg, stirring to blend. Then add pecans. Pour into pie shell. Bake at 375 degrees until top is firm and just begins to crack— about 40 minutes. Cool at least 3 hours.

LEMON MERINGUE PIE

1 and one-third cups sugar
3 tablespoons flour
1 teaspoon salt
grated lemon rind to taste
3 eggs, separated

juice of 1 lemon
1 cup boiling water
1 tablespoon butter
1 baked pie shell

Combine 1 cup sugar, flour, salt and lemon rind. Beat egg yolks; pour into saucepan. Stir in lemon juice. Add sugar mixture; mix well. Stir in boiling water. Cook until thickened, stirring constantly. Add butter; stir until melted. Pour into pie shell. Beat egg whites until firm peaks form, adding remaining sugar. Spread over lemon filling. Bake at 325 degrees for 20 minutes or until golden brown.

RHUBARB-DATE PUDDING

2 cups diced rhubarb
1 cup chopped pitted dates
½ cup sugar

1 cup soft bread crumbs
1 teaspoon butter
6 marshmallows, quartered

Cook rhubarb, dates and ¼ cup water 10 minutes. Add next 3 ingredients and put in buttered 1-quart casserole. Top with marshmallows and bake at 350 degrees for about 20 minutes. Makes 4 servings.

PINEAPPLE DESSERT

Combine and chill several hours:

½ pound miniature marshmallows
1 small bottle maraschino cherries,
    chopped

2½ cups crushed pineapple

Whip: ½ cup heavy cream. Add whipped cream to fruit mixture.

STRAWBERRIES DELUXE

Wash and hull fresh strawberries. Put in serving bowl and top with dairy sour cream. Sift light-brown sugar over cream.

INDIVIDUAL STRAWBERRY SHORTCAKES

2 cups flour
½ teaspoon salt
½ cup butter
1 cup milk

3 teaspoons baking powder
6 tablespoons (about) sugar
1 egg
sliced sweetened strawberries

Sift flour, baking powder and salt together. Combine sugar, butter, and egg; mix until creamy. Add milk, beat well. Add dry ingredients; stir well. Pour into small individual pans. Bake at 375 degrees for 15 to 20 minutes or until light brown. Spoon strawberries over warm shortcakes. Serve with whipped cream or milk. Makes 8 - 12 servings.

BUTTERSCOTCH PUDDING

First layer:

1 cup flour   ½ cup nuts
½ cup oleo

Mix, put in loaf pan and bake at 300 degrees 5 to 8 minutes.

Second layer:

Mix 1 large cake cream cheese, 1 cup powdered sugar, 1 cup Cool Whip. Put on top of first layer.

Third layer:

2 boxes of Jello pudding (any flavor) using only 3 cups of milk, boil.

Fourth layer:

Rest of Cool Whip and toasted coconut. Put on top. Chill.

BAKED ROSY RHUBARB

Cut 1 pound unpeeled rhubarb in 1" lengths. Mix in shallow baking dish, with 1 cup sugar and ¼ cup water. Bake in moderate oven (350 degrees) for 35 minutes, or until rhubarb is just tender. Chill, serve. Serves 4.

GERMAN PEACH CREAM KUCHEN

2 cups sifted flour   1 No. 2½ can peach slices, drained
¾ cup sugar   1 teaspoon cinnamon
¼ teaspoon baking powder   2 egg yolks, beaten
1 teaspoon salt   1 cup sour cream
½ cup butter or margarine

Sift flour, ¼ cup sugar, baking powder and salt together; cut in butter until mixture resembles fine crumbs. Press firmly against bottom and side of lightly greased 9" springform pan. Arrange peaches evenly over crumbs. Combine remaining sugar and cinnamon; sprinkle over peaches. Bake at 400 degrees for 15 minutes. Blend egg yolks and sour cream. Spoon over peaches. Bake for 20 minutes longer or until golden brown. Serve warm or chilled. Makes 8 servings.

STRAWBERRY SHORTCAKE

3 cups sifted all-purpose flour
3¼ teaspoons double-acting baking
    powder
sugar
1¼ teaspoons salt
heavy cream

½ cup soft shortening
1 egg, well beaten
two-thirds cup milk (about)
3 pints strawberries, washed and
    hulled

Sift flour, baking powder, 3 tablespoons sugar and the salt into bowl; cut in shortening. Add egg and enough milk to make a soft dough, mixing with fork. Knead lightly about 20 turns on floured board. Divide in thirds. Pat out thirds in greased 9" round layer-cake pans. Bake at 450 degrees about 15 minutes. Cut berries in half and sweeten to taste. Put shortcake layers together with berries between and on top. Serve with cream. Serves 6 to 8.

GRAHAM CRACKER FLUFF

Filling:

Soak: 1 package gelatine in one-third cup cold water
Mix: ½ cup sugar, ¾ cup rich milk and 2 egg yolks
Cook for one minute, stirring all the time. Remove from heat; add gelatine and 1 teaspoon vanilla. Chill until mixture begins to thicken. Then add 2 stiffly beaten egg whites and 1 cup cream whipped.

Crumbs:

Melt 1½ tablespoons butter and 3 tablespoons brown sugar together. Mix with 12 crushed graham crackers. Line the bottom of a dish with ½ of the crumbs and pour in pudding. Put remaining crumbs on top. Set in a cool place to chill.

SOUR-CREAM CHEESECAKE WITH STRAWBERRIES

1 pound soft cream cheese
granulated sugar
3 eggs
¼ teaspoon salt
½ teaspoon almond extract

1 cup sour cream
½ teaspoon vanilla extract
1 pint strawberries, washed and
    hulled
confectioners' sugar

Beat cream cheese until smooth. Gradually beat two-thirds cup granulated sugar. Beat in eggs, one at a time. Blend in salt and almond extract; beat until thick and lemon-colored. Pour into greased 9" pie pan. Bake at 350 degrees for 30 minutes. Remove; cool 20 minutes. Mix sour cream with 1 tablespoon granulated sugar and the vanilla. Beat until smooth. Pour over cooled cake; return to 350-degree oven and bake 10 minutes. Cool and decorate with strawberries dipped in confectioners' sugar. Makes 6 servings.

SPICY APPLE BREAD PUDDING

2½ cups thinly sliced apples
½ cup packed brown sugar
½ cup finely chopped nuts
1 teaspoon cinnamon
2½ cups milk, scalded
2 cups crust-trimmed white-
    bread cubes
  cream

½ teaspoon ginger
dash of salt
¼ cup granulated sugar
¼ cup molasses
½ cup raisins
2 eggs, slightly beaten
½ teaspoon vanilla extract

Mix apples, brown sugar, ¼ cup nuts and ½ teaspoon cinnamon. Put in buttered 2-quart casserole. Mix milk and bread cubes. Mix remaining nuts and cinnamon and other ingredients, except cream; stir into milk mixture. Spoon onto mixture in casserole. Set in pan of warm water and bake at 350 degrees for 50 to 60 minutes. Serve warm with cream. Makes 6 to 8 servings.

COFFEE-DATE PUDDING CAKE

3 cups chopped dates
2 cups coffee
½ cup vegetable oil
½ teaspoon each salt and ground cloves

1 teaspoon cinnamon
1 cup sugar
2 teaspoons baking soda
2 cups all-purpose flour

In skillet, combine all ingredients, except last 2, bring to boil and boil 5 minutes. Remove from heat and stir in soda, then add flour and mix well. Bake at 325 degrees for 45 minutes, or until done. Let stand in pan 10 minutes, then loosen from sides of pan and turn out on plate. Serve warm. This is a very moist pudding-like cake.

COFFEE BREAD PUDDING

1 cup strong coffee
1 cup light cream
2 cups milk
6 thin slices raisin bread
softened butter or margarine
2 eggs

½ cup sugar
½ teaspoon salt
1 teaspoon vanilla extract
¼ teaspoon nutmeg
plain or whipped cream

Bring first 3 ingredients to scalding. Spread bread lightly with butter and cut in ½" cubes (do not trim crusts). Add to first mixture. Beat eggs with sugar and salt, add bread mixture and vanilla and pour into 1½ quart casserole. Sprinkle with nutmeg. Set casserole in pan of warm water and bake at 325 degrees for 1 hour and 15 minutes, or until knife comes out clean. Serve slightly warm or chilled, with cream. Makes 8 servings.

CRAZY DATE PUDDING

Mix:

2 cups brown sugar   4 tablespoons butter
½ teaspoon salt   ½ cup butter

   Boil together 2 or 3 minutes and set aside. Into a mixing bowl put 2 cups
sifted flour, 2 cups white sugar, 4 teaspoons baking powder, ¼ teaspoon salt,
2 cups chopped dates, 1 cup chopped walnuts. Mix with 1 cup sweet milk.
Spread dough evenly in a large long baking dish and pour the first mixture on
top. Bake 45 minutes at 350 degrees. Cool and cut in squares. Top with
whipped cream.

COTTAGE PUDDING

3 eggs   1½ cups milk
lard, size of an egg   3 cups flour
¾ cup sugar   3 teaspoons baking powder
½ teaspoon salt

   Stir lard until creamy, and mix with sugar, stir eggs one at a time beating
thoroughly after each addition. Sift flour with baking powder and salt; add
alternately with milk, into creamed mixture. Bake at 400 degrees.

FRUITMALLOW SAUCE

1½ cups fruit cocktail   1 cup marshmallow creme
one-third cup milk

   Combine marshmallow creme and milk. Whip with beater until fluffy; lightly
fold in fruit cocktail; chill. Spoon over cake or gelatin desserts. Makes about
2¾ cups.

APPLE-RAISIN BROWN BETTY

2½ cups packed soft stale-bread cubes   ½ teaspoon cinnamon
4 cups finely chopped tart apples   ¼ cup butter or margarine, melted
¾ cup seedless raisins   2 tablespoons lemon juice
two-thirds cup packed brown sugar   cream
¼ teaspoon nutmeg

   Sprinkle one-third of bread cubes in greased 1½-quart casserole. Mix next
5 ingredients. Spread half the mixture on top of bread and repeat layers. Cover
with remaining bread. Drizzle with butter mixed with juice and one-third cup
water. Cover and bake at 375 degrees for 40 minutes. Uncover and bake 20
minutes longer. Serve warm with cream. Serves 6.

RHUBARB PUDDING

Cut up about one pound of unpeeled rhubarb. Place in 9 x 12" granite pan. Cover with one cup sugar and let stand while you mix:

1 cup sugar	2 eggs
1 cup sour cream	1 teaspoon soda
pinch of salt	¾ cup flour, to make a thin batter

Pour batter over rhubarb, bake at 350 degrees about 30 minutes or until a nice brown. Serve with cream or vanilla sauce, or plain.

RHUBARB CRUMBLE

4 cups diced fresh rhubarb	1 cup quick-cooking rolled oats
¼ cup orange juice	¼ teaspoon baking powder
½ cup packed brown sugar	one-third cup butter or margarine
½ cup granulated sugar	cream (optional)
½ cup flour	

Arrange rhubarb in 12 x 8" baking dish. Drizzle orange juice over fruit. Mix next 5 ingredients and cut in butter. Sprinkle on rhubarb and bake at 350 degrees about 35 minutes. Serve with cream, if desired. Serves 6 to 8.

CHEESECAKE WITH STRAWBERRY TOPPING

two-thirds cup fine graham-cracker crumbs	½ teaspoon salt
	3 eggs
2 tablespoons softened butter or margarine	2½ cups plain yogurt
	½ cup evaporated milk
sugar	juice and grated rind of 1 lemon
1 package (8 ounces) cream cheese, softened	cinnamon
	nutmeg
2 tablespoons flour	strawberry topping

Mix crumbs, butter and 2 tablespoons sugar. Press on bottom of 9" spring-form pan. Beat ¾ cup sugar, the cheese, flour and salt together. Add eggs one at a time, beating well after each addition. Blend in 2 cups yogurt and next 2 ingredients. Pour into lined pan and sprinkle with spices. Bake at 300 degrees for 50 minutes, or until firm. Make a 1" border of remaining yogurt around edge of cake. Sprinkle border with sugar and bake 8 minutes longer. Fill center with topping and chill.

STRAWBERRY TOPPING. In saucepan, mix ¾ cup sliced strawberries, 1 cup sugar, 3 tablespoons cornstarch, dash of salt and ½ cup water. Cook, stirring, until thickened. Add a few drops of red food coloring, if desired. Cool.

BROWN SUGAR PUDDING

2 cups brown sugar
2 tablespoons butter
1 cup flour

½ cup sugar
3 teaspoons baking powder

Combine brown sugar, 1 cup water and butter in saucepan; bring to a boil. Cook, stirring until brown sugar is dissolved. Pour into 8" square pan. Mix flour, sugar, baking powder and ½ cup water; pour into syrup. Do not stir. Bake at 350 degrees for 15 to 20 minutes. Serve slightly warm; top with whipped cream if desired.

EXTRA CREAMY CHEESECAKE

1 pound cream cheese
salt
½ teaspoon almond extract
1 teaspoon vanilla extract

sugar
3 eggs
1 cup dairy sour cream

Beat cheese until fluffy. Gradually beat in two-thirds cup sugar and a dash of salt. Add eggs one at a time, beating well after each. Beat until smooth. Add almond flavoring and pour into buttered 9" pie-pan. Bake at 350 degrees for 25 minutes. Remove from oven and let cool away from drafts 20 minutes. While cake is cooling, beat together sour cream, 3 tablespoons sugar, a dash of salt and the vanilla. Pour over top of cake. Return to oven and bake 10 minutes longer. Cool. Serves 7 or 8.

BAKED APPLE DUMPLINGS

½ recipe pastry
6 medium-size tart cooking apples
1¾ teaspoons ground cinnamon

1½ cups sugar
¼ cup butter or margarine
cream or whipped cream

Roll pastry to a little less than one-eighth" thickness and cut in six 7" squares. Peel and core apples. Bring to boil 1 cup sugar, 2 cups water, 3 tablespoons butter and ¼ teaspoon cinnamon. Put an apple on each square of pastry. Mix remaining sugar and cinnamon and use to fill apple cavities. Dot with remaining butter. Bring opposite points of pastry up over apple. Overlap, moisten and seal. Lift carefully and put a few inches apart in baking dish. Pour hot syrup around dumplings. Bake at 425 degrees for 40 minutes, or until crust is well browned and apples are tender. Serve warm with cream. Makes 6 servings.

INDIAN PUDDING

½ cup cornmeal
4 cups hot milk
¾ cup light molasses
2 eggs
2 tablespoons butter

¼ cup brown sugar
1 teaspoon salt
1 teaspoon cinnamon
½ teaspoon ginger
1 cup cold milk

Slowly stir cornmeal into hot milk in double boiler top. Cook over boiling water, stirring occasionally, 20 minutes. Grease bottom of 12 x 8 x 2" baking dish. To cornmeal, add rest of ingredients, except cold milk; mix well. Turn into prepared dish; add milk. Bake, uncovered in 350-degree oven for 50 minutes or until set. Serve hot, with ice cream. Makes 8 servings.

PLAIN BREAD PUDDING

2 cups dry bread crumbs
4 cups hot milk
½ cup sugar
3 eggs, beaten
4 tablespoons melted margarine

½ teaspoon salt
1 teaspoon vanilla
¾ cup raisins
¼ teaspoon nutmeg
¼ teaspoon cinnamon

Add bread crumbs to hot milk; set aside to cool. Add remaining ingredients; pour into buttered pan. Place pudding in pan of hot water. Bake for 1 hour at 350 degrees.

APPLE CRISP

4 cups thinly sliced peeled cooking
   apples
½ cup packed light-brown sugar
2 tablespoons lemon juice
1 cup all-purpose flour
¾ cup granulated sugar
1 teaspoon baking powder

½ teaspoon salt
1 egg, slightly beaten
one-third cup butter or margarine
   melted and cooled
½ teaspoon cinnamon
cream

Mix first 3 ingredients and arrange in shallow baking dish about 10" x 6" x 2". Mix next 4 ingredients. Add egg and mix until crumbly. Sprinkle on mixture in dish. Drizzle with butter and sprinkle with cinnamon. Bake at 350 degrees about 35 minutes. Serve warm with cream. Makes 6 servings.

STOVE-TOP CHOCOLATE BREAD PUDDING

1 square unsweetened chocolate
1½ cups milk
2 cups crust-trimmed white-bread
   cubes
¼ cup sugar
one-eighth teaspoon salt

1 teaspoon vanilla extract
8 large marshmallows, quartered, or
   2 ounces miniature marshmallows
cream (optional)

    Melt chocolate in milk in top part of double boiler over simmering water. Add next 4 ingredients and cook, stirring, until thickened. Remove from heat and stir in vanilla and marshmallows. Serve warm, with cream, if desired. Serves 4.

LEMON BREAD PUDDING

2 cups crust-trimmed white-bread
   cubes
¾ cup sugar
juice and grated rind of 1 lemon

½ cup butter, melted
4 eggs, separated
two-thirds cup milk
cream flavored with nutmeg
   (optional)

    Mix first 3 ingredients, then stir in butter. Beat egg yolks until thick and lemon-colored. Add milk and pour over bread mixture. Fold in stiffly beaten egg whites. Pour into buttered 1½-quart casserole. Bake in moderate oven (350 degrees) about 30 minutes. Serve warm, with cream, if desired. Makes 6 servings.

RHUBARB CRUNCH

1 cup flour
¾ cup oatmeal
½ cup shortening

1 cup brown sugar
1 teaspoon cinnamon

    Mix all above together until crumbly; press half of mixture in bottom of 9″ baking pan. Put 5 cups diced rhubarb over crumbs.

Combine:

1 cup sugar
1½ cups water
red food coloring

2 tablespoons cornstarch
1 teaspoon vanilla

    Cook this mixture until it is thick and clear, then pour over rhubarb in baking pan. Top with remaining crumbs and bake at 350 degrees for 1 hour. (if pyrex pan is used set oven at 325 degrees). Serve warm or cold with whipped cream or ice cream.

TOPSY-TURVY CHERRY PUDDING

1¼ cups sugar
2 tablespoons butter
1 cup sifted flour
one-eighth teaspoon salt
1 teaspoon baking powder

¾ cup milk
1 can (1 pound) red sour cherries,
    drained
½ cup cherry juice
whipped cream or ice cream

Cream 1 cup of the sugar with butter. Sift flour, measure and sift with salt and baking powder; add alternately with milk to butter mixture. Pour into a buttered shallow baking dish. Combine cherries with remaining ¼ cup sugar and cherry juice. Heat to boiling point. Pour over batter. Bake at 350 degrees for 30 minutes. Serve with cream or ice cream. Serves 6.

PEACH CRISP

6 to 7 large peaches
juice 1 lemon
1 cup sifted flour

1 cup brown sugar, packed
½ cup margarine

Put peeled, sliced peaches in shallow 2-quart baking dish and sprinkle with lemon juice. Mix flour and brown sugar. Cut in margarine with pastry blender or fingers until crumbly. Press over peaches. Bake at 375 degrees for 25 minutes, or until peaches are tender. Serve warm with cream. Makes 6 servings.

STRAWBERRY COBBLECAKE

1 pint strawberries
2 cups sifted regular flour
2 teaspoons baking powder
½ teaspoon salt
1 cup firmly packed light brown sugar

8 tablespoons (1 stick) butter or
    margarine
1 egg
milk
1 tablespoon granulated sugar
cream

Wash strawberries, hull, and halve. Sift flour, baking powder, and salt into a large bowl; stir in brown sugar. Cut in 6 tablespoons of the butter or margarine with a pastry blender until mixture is crumbly. Beat egg slightly in a 1-cup measure; add milk to make 1 cup. Stir into flour mixture until well blended; pour into a greased deep 9" pie plate. Arrange strawberries, cut side down, in rings on top; dot with remaining 2 tablespoons butter or margarine; sprinkle with granulated sugar. Bake at 350 degrees for 50 minutes, or until firm in center. Cut in wedges; serve warm with cream. Makes 6 to 8 servings.

SALADS

AND RELISHES

INDEX FOR SALADS AND RELISHES

CUCUMBER SALAD

1 6-oz. package lemon Jello
1 tablespoon vinegar
1 medium onion, chopped
1 cup salad dressing

1 cup boiling water
1 medium cucumber, chopped
1 carton small curd cottage cheese
½ cup chopped walnuts

Dissolve Jello in boiling water; stir vinegar. Chill until partially congealed.
Add remaining ingredients; mix well. Place in dish or mold; chill until firm.
Makes 8 servings.

BANANA DRESSING

(for fruit or Jello salads, good with fruit.)

1 ripe banana, mashed
½ cup mayonnaise

1 tablespoon lemon juice
¼ cup milk

Mix together banana and lemon juice. Stir in mayonnaise and milk. Makes
about 1¼ cups. Add additional milk for thinner consistency, if desired.

FROZEN SALAD

1 cup Miracle Whip salad dressing
1 8-oz. package cream cheese
1 cup drained pineapple tidbits
1 cup chopped, drained apricots
1 cup heavy cream, whipped

½ cup chopped maraschino cherries
2 tablespoons confectioners' sugar
Few drops red food coloring
2 cups miniature marshmallows

Gradually add salad dressing to softened cream cheese, mixing until well
blended. Stir in fruit, sugar, and food coloring. Fold in marshmallows and
whipped cream. Pour into 9 x 5" loaf pan; freeze. Unmold on platter.
10 to 12 servings.

JELLO SALAD

1 package lemon Jello
1 package lime Jello
2 cups hot water
1 cup Miracle Whip
2 tablespoons horseradish

No. 2 can crushed pineapple
½ cup milk
1 cup nut meats
1 cup cottage cheese

Mix Jello and hot water. When cool add pineapple. When slightly
congealed, add milk, nuts, and cottage cheese, horseradish, and Miracle
Whip salad dressing, Serves 12-16.

APPLE SALTED PEANUT SALAD

4 cups apples cubed (not pared)
1 cup sliced bananas
mayonnaise

1 cup chopped celery
1 cup salted peanuts, chopped
lettuce

Mix lightly fruit, nuts, etc., blend with mayonnaise to moisten. Arrange on crisp lettuce.

5-WAY SALAD

1 cup sour cream
1 cup mandarin orange segments
1 cup diced or miniature marshmallows

1 cup coconut
1 cup crushed pineapple

Mix all 5 together and refrigerate 24 hours before serving.

FAMILY COLESLAW

1 cup vinegar
½ cup water
1 quart shredded cabbage
½ cup grated carrot
1 cup chopped celery

1 cup sugar
1 teaspoon prepared mustard
½ cup chopped green pepper
1 tablespoon salt

Combine vinegar, sugar, water and mustard in saucepan; bring to a boil. Cool. Combine cabbage, green pepper, carrot and salt in large bowl; cover with ice water. Soak until vegetables are chilled; drain. Add celery to cabbage mixture. Cover with cooled dressing; refrigerate. May be stored in refrigerator for several days.

APPLE SALAD

Chop apples, as many as you want, 2 stalks celery, 1 cup nuts.

Dressing:

1 cup granulated sugar
3 teaspoons flour

1 egg, beaten

Stir this together with water. Add 1 cup of water and boil. When done, add a little vinegar and salt. Let it cool before pouring over apples. Add ½ pint cream, whipped.

HOT POTATO SALAD

It has a bacon mustard dressing.

2 slices bacon
1 onion, chopped
1 tablespoon flour
¼ cup vinegar
½ cup water
1 teaspoon sugar

one eighth teaspoon pepper
3 tablespoons prepared mustard
5 cups sliced, cooked potato
Chopped parsley
½ teaspoon salt

Mince bacon and fry until crisp; remove. Cook onion in bacon fat until lightly browned. Blend in flour; add bacon, vinegar, water, and seasonings; bring to boil. Add potato, mixing lightly; heat. Sprinkle with parsley and serve. Or let cool, store in refrigerator, and reheat before serving. Serves 4

SUPPER SALAD BOWL

5 cups shredded cabbage
1 cucumber, sliced
¾ cup bologna sausage (cubes)
½ green pepper, diced
½ cup French dressing

3 large tomatoes, sliced
1 onion, chopped or sliced into
    separate rings
1 can kidney beans, drained
½ cup mayonnaise

Add dressing and mayonnaise tossing until well blended.

MOLDED FRUIT SALAD

1 3-oz. package lemon Jello
1 3-oz. package orange Jello
2 cups boiling water
1 cup cold water
1 cup syrup from apricots
2 cups (1 lb. 14-oz. can) drained
apricots

1 cup (13½-oz. can) drained
    pineapple tidbits
3 cups miniature marshmallows
lettuce
fruit cheese dressing
¾ cup shredded sharp cheddar
    cheese

Dissolve lemon and orange Jello in boiling water; add cold water and syrup. Chill until almost firm; fold in fruit and marshmallows. Pour into 2½-quart mold. Chill until firm. Unmold on lettuce. Top with fruit cheese dressing; sprinkle with cheese. Fruit Cheese Dressing: Gradually add two-thirds cup syrup from pineapple to 1 tablespoon flour; stir in one beaten egg. Cook over low heat until thickened; chill. Fold in 1 cup of heavy cream, whipped. 12 servings.

CORN RELISH

12 ears corn
4 medium onions, peeled
3 tablespoons salt
1 teaspoon tumeric powder
1 tablespoon mustard

1 small head cabbage
3 sweet red peppers, seeded
3 tablespoons flour
2¼ cups sugar
1 quart vinegar

Cut corn from cob. Put cabbage, onions, and peppers through food chopper, using coarse blade. Combine all vegetabl es. Blend salt, flour,turmeric, sugar and mustard. Add vinegar and vegetables. Bring to boil and simmer 25 to 30 minutes Seal at once in hot sterilized jars. Makes about 8 pints.

PICKLED GARDEN RELISH

1 small head cauliflower, broken in
   flowerets and sliced
2 stalks celery, cut in 1" pieces
1 jar (2 ounces) pimiento-stuffed
   olives, drained
½ cup salad oil
1 teaspoon salt
1 jar (4 ounces) pimientos drained
   and cut in strips

2 medium carrots, cut in medium
   2" strips
1 green pepper, cut in medium 2"
   strips
¾ cup wine vinegar
2 tablespoons sugar
¼ teaspoon pepper

Combine all ingredients and ½ cup water in large skillet. Bring to boil, stirring occasionally. Cover and simmer 5 to 7 minutes. Cool. Refrigerate, covered, about 24 hours, before serving. Will keep refrigerated, at least one week. Makes about 2 quarts.

7-UP SALAD

2 packages lemon Jello
2 cups boiling water
2 cups 7-up
2 cups miniature marshmallows

4 large bananas
1 can pineapple tidbits, drained
nuts

Topping:

1 cup pineapple juice
1 tablespoon cornstarch
1 tablespoon lemon juice

2 eggs, beaten
1 envelope Dream Whip

Blend pineapple juice, cornstarch, eggs, and lemon juice. Beat smooth and cook over low heat, stirring constantly until thickened. Cool. Fold in Dream Whip; spread over Jello.

COMPANY SALAD

1 box lemon Jello
1 jar Kraft pimiento cheese
1½ cups boiling water

1 can pineapple
½ pint whipped cream

Mix Jello and water, let set till it is like jelly. Whip until blended. Combine cheese and pineapple and mix with Jello and fold in whipped cream. Put in greased baking dish and refrigerate.

CRANBERRY ORANGE RELISH

Pick and wash 1 lb. fresh cranberries (2 cups). Combine with 2 cups sugar, ½ cup each water and orange juice and 1 tablespoon grated orange rind, in a medium saucepan. Cook, stirring often, 10 minutes, or just until cranberries pop. Cool relish, then chill. Makes 3 cups.

CARROT AND RAISIN SALAD

½ cup raisins
1 tablespoon orange juice
1 teaspoon grated orange peel

½ cup mayonnaise
1 teaspoon lemon juice
3 cups grated carrots

Cover raisins with warm water; soak until plump. Drain. Mix mayonnaise with raisins, juices and orange peel. Add to carrots; toss lightly with fork. Serve on salad greens. Makes 6 servings.

KIDNEY BEAN SALAD

1 cup red kidney beans
2 chopped hard cooked eggs
2 tablespoons chopped pimiento
1 teaspoon salt
¼ teaspoon paprika

½ cup chopped celery
2 tablespoons sweet pickle, chopped
1 tablespoon finely chopped onion
½ cup mayonnaise or French dressing

Mix all together and garnish with extra dressing if desired.

TOMATO RELISH

6 ripe tomatoes, peeled and sliced
3 medium sweet onions, peeled and sliced
½ cup water
½ teaspoon salt

3 cucumbers, peeled and sliced
one third cup cider vinegar
¼ cup sugar
¼ teaspoon pepper

Alternate slices of tomatoes, cucumbers, and onions in large bowl. Combine remaining ingredients and shake well; pour over vegetables. Refrigerate 24 hours, turning once or twice to distribute flavor

GREEN TOMATO CHOW

6 quart basket green tomatoes   3 pounds onions

Cut up tomatoes and cover with ½ cup coarse salt at night. In morning, drain. Cut up in small pieces two red peppers and two green peppers, then 4 cups white sugar and 1 quart white vinegar. Also add one tablespoon pickling spices in bag. Boil for one hour or more. Put in bottles and seal while hot.

CABBAGE SALAD

In one large bowl, dice 3 stalks celery, one onion, one mango, shred 4 cups cabbage, slice fine 2 carrots. Dressing: ½ cup salad oil, 1 cup sugar, ½ cup vinegar, 1 teaspoon salt, ½ cup water, 1 teaspoon celery seed.

KITCHEN VEGETABLE SALAD

(Keeps several weeks)

Cook until thick:

2 tablespoons flour
1 cup sugar

¾ cup vinegar
¼ cup water

Remove from heat and add 2 teaspoons prepared mustard. Set aside to cool. Cook 2 packages mixed vegetables and a little onion. Drain. Also drain 1 can red kidney beans. Dice 1 cup celery, ½ cup green pepper mango. Add cooled sauce, mix well together and store in refrigerator.

HOT POTATO SALAD

8 freshly boiled potatoes, diced while hot
2 medium onions, chopped
½ cup vinegar, or vinegar and water if a milder dressing is desired

4 hard-cooked eggs, chopped while hot
8-10 slices of bacon, sliced
salt and pepper
little sugar, if desired

Place bacon in skillet and fry until light brown. Add seasonings and vinegar. Boil up and pour over potatoes, eggs, and onions which have been tossed together. Heat through and serve.

BANANA-CABBAGE SLAW

½ medium head cabbage, shredded
2 tablespoons sugar
2 to 3 bananas, sliced

½ cup mayonnaise
1 tablespoon milk

Place cabbage in salad bowl. Combine mayonnaise, sugar and milk; mix well. Pour over cabbage. Add bananas; toss lightly. Serve immediately. Makes 6 servings.

CUCUMBERS, RADISHES AND ONIONS IN SOUR CREAM

Put in bowl 2 sliced peeled cucumbers, 8 sliced radishes and 2 sliced peeled onions. Mix ¾ cup dairy sour cream, ¼ cup vinegar and ½ teaspoon steak sauce. Add seasoned salt and pepper to taste, pour over vegetables; toss lightly. Serves 6.

HOT MASHED-POTATO SALAD

¾ cup mayonnaise-pickle sandwich spread
¼ teaspoon pepper
3 green onions, finely sliced
¾ cup finely chopped celery
1 jar (2 ounces) chopped pimiento, drained

1 teaspoon salt
5 servings mashed potatoes
¼ cup chopped green pepper
1 teaspoon prepared mustard
2 eggs, hard-cooked and chopped

Bring 1½ cups water to boil. Add sandwich spread, salt and pepper. Gradually add potatoes, beating with fork until well mixed. Mix in remaining ingredients, except last 2. Then fold in pimiento and eggs. Serve hot. Good with frankfurters. Makes 6 servings.

CHERRY CREAM SQUARES

2 3-oz. packages cherry Jello
3 bananas, sliced
½ cup chopped nuts

2 cups miniature marshmallows
1 cup dairy sour cream

Prepare cherry Jello as directed on package; chill until almost firm. Fold in bananas; pour into 8-inch square pan. Chill until firm. Combine marshmallows and sour cream; spread on Jello Top with nuts. Chill. 6 servings.

ENVY SALAD

1 large box lemon Jello
1 large package cream cheese
2 tablespoons sugar
1 10-oz. bottle lemon-lime carbonated
    beverage

1 + one-third cups hot water
1 small can crushed pineapple
1 teaspoon vanilla
½ cup chopped pecans
2 drops of green food coloring

Dissolve gelatin in hot water in mixer bowl; add cream cheese. Beat at medium speed until blended. Stir in remaining ingredients by hand. Pour into mold; chill until firm.

APRICOT SALAD

2 packages orange Jello (dissolved in
    2 cups hot water)
1 (29 oz.) can apricots

1 large can crushed pineapple

Drain apricots and pineapple and add 1 cup of mixed juice to Jello. Whip apricots and mix with pineapple and add to Jello Chill.

HOT CORN SLAW

1 can whole kernel corn
5 slices bacon
2 teaspoons sugar
1 teaspoon salt

3 cups shredded red & green cabbage
½ teaspoon celery seed
3 tablespoons vinegar

Fry bacon until crisp; drain on paper towel. Add ¼ cup corn liquid, sugar, salt, and cabbage to bacon fat; cook until tender. Add celery seed, vinegar, crumbled bacon and drained corn; heat. Makes 6 to 7 servings.

FROZEN FRUIT SALAD

1 egg, beaten
¼ cup sugar
2½ tablespoons flour
2 tablespoons vinegar
1 can crushed pineapple (drained)

1 cup whipped cream
1 can pears, diced
3 bananas, mashed
12 cherries

Mix egg, sugar, flour, and salt, vinegar and pineapple juice. Cook until thick, stirring constantly. Cool. Then fold in whipped cream, add pineapple, pears, bananas, and cherries and freeze.

SPECIAL CABBAGE SALAD

4 cups shredded cabbage
2 tablespoons sugar
dash of pepper
2 hard-cooked eggs, sliced

½ cup light cream
1 teaspoon salt
2 tablespoons vinegar

Heap cabbage in bowl. Combine cream, sugar, salt, pepper and vinegar. Pour over cabbage; toss lightly. Arrange egg white rings around rim of bowl, sieved yolk in center for special trim. 6 servings.

PARADISE SALAD

First layer:

1 package cherry Jello dissolved in 1½ cups hot water, 1 cup diced apples. Mix diced apples into Jello and chill.

Second layer:

1 package lemon Jello
2 (3 ounce) packages cream cheese

1 large can crushed pineapple
1 cup chopped nuts

Drain the pineapple. Keep the fruit for the third layer. Heat the juice and dissolve the lemon Jello in it. Then mix with cream cheese until it is melted. Cool, then add nuts and pour over first layer and chill again.

Third layer:

1 package lime

1 cup hot water

When Jello is dissolved add crushed pineapple, cool and pour over second layer. Chill overnight.

LAST OF THE GARDEN

Mix together:

1 can yellow beans, drained
1 can kidney beans, drained
1 diced green mango
½ cup diced onion

1 can green beans, drained
1 cup diced celery
½ cup pimiento, or 1 can

Bring to a boil and pour over vegetables:

1½ cups sugar
1 cup water

1 cup vinegar

Let set for 24 hours.

CANDY,
ICE CREAM,
AND MISC.

INDEX FOR CANDIES AND ICE CREAMS

NUTS AND BOLTS

Preheat oven to 250 degrees and combine:

6 tablespoons butter or margarine
4 teaspoons Worcestershire sauce
three-eighths teaspoon garlic powder

6 cups Chex (Mix Corn, Wheat, and
   Rice equally or any way you like!)
1 jar Planters Dry Roasted Peanuts

Pour melted butter into shallow baking pan. Stir in Worcestershire sauce and garlic powder. Add Chex and Planters Dry Roasted Peanuts. Mix until all pieces are coated. Heat in 250-degree oven 45 minutes. Stir every 15 minutes. Spread on absorbent paper to cool. Makes 8 cups.

SPICED INSTANT TEA MIX

1 cup lemon flavored instant tea
2 cups Tang
3 cups sugar

1 teaspoon cinnamon
1 teaspoon ground cloves

To use mix about 3 tablespoons of dry mix to 1 cup of hot water. (Good iced, too). Mix may be stored in air tight container for later use. (The amount of sugar is more than some might like, may be reduced.)

HOT COCOA

For each serving, mix in saucepan 1 tablespoon each cocoa and sugar, dash salt and ¼ cup water. Bring to boil and cook until thickened. Add ¾ cup undiluted evaporated milk and heat until scalded. Add a few drops vanilla. Top with whipped cream or a marshmallow.

PEANUT BUTTER FUDGE

1 cup sugar
1 cup (packed) brown sugar
two-thirds cup evaporated milk
¼ cup butter or margarine

½ cup peanut butter
1   7-oz. jar marshmallow creme
2 teaspoons vanilla

Combine sugars, milk and butter in saucepan. Bring to a boil, stirring frequently. Cook to soft-ball stage, 238 degrees on candy thermometer, stirring occasionally. Add peanut butter, marshmallow creme and vanilla; stir to blend thoroughly. Pour into greased 8-inch square pan; refrigerate until firm. Cut into squares.

PEANUT BUTTER FUDGE SAUCE

1 cup quick chocolate flavored milk
¼ cup creamy peanut butter
one-third cup milk

3 tablespoons light corn syrup
2 tablespoons butter

In 1-quart saucepan combine chocolate mix, peanut butter, milk and corn syrup. Bring to a full boil over low heat; stirring constantly. Remove from heat; stir in butter. Serve warm or cold over ice cream. Makes approximately 1 cup.

CRACKER JACK

1 cup molasses
1 cup brown sugar

1 tablespoon vinegar
2 tablespoons butter

Mix well and cook until it hardens in cold water. Then add 1 teaspoon soda. Pour over 5 to 6 quarts popcorn . Mix well. May be baked in a slow oven.

PEANUT BUTTER-MARSHMALLOW FUDGE

Cook to soft ball stage:

2 cups sugar

two-thirds cup milk

Then add:

1 cup marshmallow fluff
1 cup peanut butter

1 teaspoon vanilla

Mix well and pour in buttered pan.

SEA FOAM CANDY

3 cups light brown sugar
1 cup water
2 teaspoons vinegar

2 egg whites
1 cup chopped nuts
1 teaspocn vanilla extract

Cook sugar, water and vinegar until it forms a medium ball when tested in cold water (240 degrees). Pour over stiffly beaten egg whites, beating continually. When creamy, add nuts and vanilla. When stiff, pour into buttered pan and cut into squares.

RED APPLES ON STICK

12 small red eating apples
12 wooden skewers
3 cups sugar

¾ cup light corn syrup
few drops of oil of cloves
red food coloring or 12 red cinnamon
candies

Wash apples in hot water and dry. Insert skewer in blossom end of each apple. In saucepan, mix sugar, corn syrup and 1 cup water. Cook, stirring, until sugar dissolves. Add oil of cloves and a little coloring. Continue cooking, without stirring, until small amount of mixture forms a hard piece that cracks when dropped into cold water (290 degrees on candy thermometer). Set pan over boiling water. Dip each apple into syrup, remove and whirl apple until syrup covers it smoothly. Stand apples on tray to cool and harden.

CARAMELS

1 lb. brown sugar
1 cup light Karo

1 can Eagle Brand condensed milk
1 cup butter

Boil 12 minutes stirring constantly. Pour in greased pan. Cool, cut, and wrap in waxed paper.

GREEN TOMATO MINCEMEAT

7 pounds green tomatoes
4½ cups sugar
1 tablespoon each cinnamon and
    ground cloves
½ teaspoon nutmeg
½ cup vinegar

½ teaspoon salt
½ cup ground beef suet
1 package seedless raisins
grated rind and juice of ½ orange
1½ tablespoons lemon juice

Wash and trim tomatoes. Chop fine or force through coarse blade of food chopper. Drain off liquid and cover tomatoes with cold water. Drain again and cover with boiling water. Drain well and put in kettle with remaining ingredients. Bring to boil and simmer, uncovered, stirring occasionally, 20 to 25 minutes, or until thick. Pour into hot sterilized jars and seal. Makes about 5 pints, or enough for 3 to 4 pies. For pie: Put 3 cups mincemeat in pastry-lined 9"pie pan. Dot with 1 to 2 tablespoons butter. Adjust top crust and bake in hot oven (425 degrees) about 30 minutes.

COUNTRY VANILLA ICE CREAM

No cooking, just eggs to beat and milk to measure.

4 eggs	4 cups heavy cream
2¼ cups sugar	4½ teaspoons vanilla
5 cups milk	½ teaspoon salt

Add sugar gradually to beaten eggs. Continue to beat until mixture is very stiff. Add remaining ingredients and mix thoroughly. Pour into gallon freezer and freeze as directed for your ice-cream freezer. Makes 4 quarts. Serves 12 - 16 people.

CHOCOLATE CANDY

Here is an easy candy recipe. It is rich.

1½ cups chocolate chips	3 tablespoons oleo
½ cup peanut butter	1 bag large marshmallows

Place marshmallows in a foil-lined pan. Mix rest of ingredients in sauce pan and melt over low heat. Pour over marshmallows and chill.

ICE CREAM PIES

32 graham crackers	½ pound butter

Mix for crust. Line 2 pans and bake 10 minutes in moderate oven.

Filling:

1 package Knox gelatine	1 cup sugar
1 cup milk	2 egg yolks
	pinch of salt

Cook and cool. Beat egg whites. Whip 1 pint ice cream. Add 1 teaspoon vanilla. Mix. Then fold this with the sauce. Fill pies and chill in refrigerator.

SWEET-CHOCOLATE ICE CREAM

2 bars (4 ounces each) sweet cooking chocolate	1 cup sugar
2 cups milk	2 cups light cream
one-eighth teaspoon salt	1 tablespoon vanilla extract
3 eggs	

Put chocolate and milk in top part of double boiler over boiling water and heat, stirring, until chocolate is dissolved. Beat salted eggs and sugar; add cream and vanilla. Add chocolate mixture and strain into container of crank-type freezer. Freeze until firm. Makes about 1½ quarts.

STRAWBERRY PRESERVES

1 pint strawberries   2 cups sugar
1 tablespoon butter or margarine

Wash strawberries, hull, and halve. Place in a large heavy saucepan. Sprinkle with sugar, but do not stir in. Place pan over high heat. Watch carefully, and when juices start to flow, stir lightly just to mix berries and sugar; stir in butter or margarine. Heat to boiling; cook rapidly, stirring several times, 10 minutes; remove from heat. Pour into a small bowl. Makes about 2 cups.

CHOCOLATE FUDGE SAUCE

Heat together 1 cup milk and 4 squares unsweetened chocolate over low heat, stirring constantly. Beat until smooth. Add ¼ teaspoon salt, 2 cups sugar and ¼ cup light corn syrup. Bring to boil and cook, stirring, 5 minutes. Remove from heat and stir in 2 tablespoons butter and 1 teaspoon vanilla. Serve warm or cold on ice cream, or plain cake or pudding. Makes 2 cups.

FRUIT JELLO CANDY

Tender, clear gumdrops that are slightly softer than those you buy:

1 box powdered fruit pectin   1 cup light corn syrup
¾ cup water   10 drops orange or green food
½ teaspoon baking soda   coloring
1 cup sugar   1½ to 2 teaspoons orange extract
                                             or ½ teaspoon peppermint extract

(Or use 1 bottle liquid fruit pectin and reduce water to 2 tablespoons.)

Mix powdered fruit pectin, water, and baking soda in a 2-quart saucepan (mixture will foam slightly). Mix sugar and corn syrup in another 2-quart saucepan. Place both pans over highest heat and cook, stirring alternately, until foam disappears from pectin mixture and sugar mixture is boiling rapidly. (This takes 3 to 5 minutes.) Then pour pectin mixture in a slow, steady stream into boiling sugar mixture, stirring constantly. Boil and stir 1 minute longer. Remove from heat; stir in coloring and extract. Immediately pour into 9 x 5 inch loaf pan, 8-inch square pan, or 8-inch cake or pie pan. Let stand at room temperature until cool and firm. Cut in ¾-inch squares and roll in granulated or confectioners' sugar. (To store or package candies, let them stand overnight at room temperature to prevent weeping.) Makes about 5 dozen squares.

TOMATO JAM

3 pounds (6 large) fully ripe tomatoes
1 lemon, thinly sliced

1 box (2½ ounces) powdered fruit
pectin
5 cups sugar

Scald, peel and quarter tomatoes, removing stem and core. Remove seeds and drain off juice, reserving only pulp. Put in kettle, bring to boil and simmer, uncovered, 8 to 10 minutes. Measure; you will need 3 cups. Put tomatoes, lemon and pectin in kettle. Bring to full rolling boil, stirring constantly. Add sugar and boil rapidly 2 minutes. Cool 5 minutes, stirring occasionally to prevent floating fruit. Fill hot sterilized jars; seal. Makes 4 to 5 half-pint jars.

HARD CANDY

powdered sugar
3¾ cups sugar
1½ cups Karo light corn syrup

1 cup water
1 teaspoon desired flavoring oil
desired food coloring

Sprinkle 18 x 24 inch strip of heavy-duty aluminum foil with powdered sugar. Mix first 3 ingredients in large heavy saucepan. Stir over medium heat until sugar dissolves. Boil, without stirring, until temperature reaches 310 degrees or until drops of syrup form hard and brittle threads in cold water. Remove from heat. Stir in flavoring oil and coloring. Pour onto foil. Cool; break into pieces. Store in airtight container.

Suggested combinations of flavors and colors:

peppermint	pink
cinnamon	red
spearmint	green
lemon	yellow
wintergreen	pale green
anise	dark blue
clove	gold
orange	orange
sassafras	light brown
lime	yellow green
butter	light yellow
cherry	red
raspberry	blue red
chocolate	brown
grape	purple
butter rum	yellow brown

STRAWBERRY TOPPING

1 cup heavy cream
¼ cup confectioners' sugar

1 cup sliced strawberries
½ cup miniature marshmallows

Whip cream until almost stiff, then beat in sugar. Fold in berries and marshmallows. Serve as topping for angel food cake, ice cream or puddings. Makes 2½ cups.

POPCORN BALLS

½ pound popcorn
1 cup sugar

1 cup white corn syrup
1 3-oz. package orange gelatin

Prepare popcorn according to package directions; place in large pan. Bring sugar, syrup and gelatin to a boil in saucepan, stirring until sugar and gelatin are dissolved. Pour over popcorn, mix until popcorn is completely coated. Form balls quickly with hands; place on waxed paper. Cool. Makes 18 balls.

CARAMEL TURTLES

On greased baking sheet, arrange pecan halves, flat side down, in groups of four. Center one vanilla caramel atop each cluster of pecans. Heat in slow oven (325 degrees) till caramels soften, 7 to 8 minutes. Remove from oven; with a buttered spatula, flatten caramels over pecans. Cool slightly; remove from pan to waxed paper. Spread tops with melted semisweet chocolate pieces.

TOMATO JAM

Mix together:

2 cups apples, finely chopped
2 cups ripe tomatoes, well drained

1 cup ground orange

Add:

3 cups sugar and boil until thick. Pour into sterilized glasses and seal.

Continued from page 92